VILLARD Ⓥ NEW YORK

RABID NUN INFECTS ENTIRE CONVENT

And Other Sensational Stories from a Tabloid Writer

ALL MADE UP BY

TOM D'ANTONI

It ain't necessarily so that it ain't necessarily so.

—SUN RA

HEADLINES

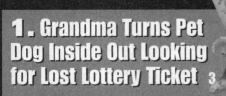

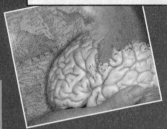
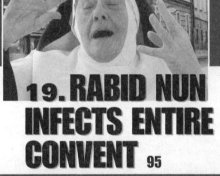

I MADE UP ALL OF THE STORIES I WROTE FOR *THE SUN,* A NATIONAL SUPERMAR-
ket tabloid newspaper. They knew it, and I'm proud of it. This is the saga of
my dive into the cesspool of my own mind. And since I made up fake by-
lines, too, never using my own name, it had been my own private cesspool
until I outed myself in front of millions of TV viewers as having done these
awful deeds.

Wait, that's too dramatic, but not by much. I mean, it isn't *The New York
Times* we're talking about. And this isn't *Shattered Glass.*

All of the facts in the narrative parts of this book are eminently check-
able. The facts in the stories came from inside my head, except for one story,
which was suggested by a guy who was cutting my hair at the time.

I have rewritten these stories, as the folks at *The Sun* rewrote my origi-
nals, which were cut (unmercifully) to fit their space and standards. Yes,
"standards." I must admit, there were some parts of these stories that were a
bit much, even for them.

The narrative was first a story for *The Oregonian* and the *Baltimore City
Paper.* Upon publication, in Portland, I was invited to be on a talk show in
Seattle. They asked me to make up a tabloid story on the spot. But they

stopped smiling when I made up a story about how there was a talk show host farm where people just like the cohosts were mass-produced from pods.

Over the years, I used the piece to introduce myself to women. It was good if they laughed, and just as good if they were horrified. Better to know at the beginning. I have read the *Oregonian* piece in public several times, and the jokes always killed. One night I was sitting around with pianist/writer David Vest, who suggested this book.

I am supposed to thank the people who influenced me to write this book and these stories. But if you had inspired this stuff, would you want to be thanked? Think about it. I can't thank deities, as athletes do. I might get struck by lightning.

I suppose I can thank poverty, drugs, and my colleague Garey Lambert, with whom I was making one of the Baltimore Orioles' pregame radio shows when I first wrote this stuff. We weren't making any money doing that show. I had to do something, so I ended up writing these stories.

We had put all the money we were making into production gear, and although I was being well fed in the Orioles press box, I did not have the "luxury" of being the projectionist at an art film theater, as Garey did.

These stories helped keep the lights on in the apartment we shared. People called us the Odd Couple. He was gay, I was straight, and one of my ex-wives lived upstairs.

Garey "edited" these stories, to some extent, but mostly he was my friend and laughed at the jokes. He was also the brother I never had.

Garey became one of the top AIDS journalists in the United States before that disease took him in 1996. There's hardly a week that goes by that I don't have the urge to call him about something. Thanks, Garey.

GRANDMA TURNS PET DOG INSIDE OUT LOOKING FOR LOST LOTTERY TICKET

1

My career as a supermarket tabloid writer ended when I was a guest on *Oprah*. This life-changing event (for me) took place in 1988 and a few of her formats, a few of her makeovers ago.

Oprah's producer called me. She was a drinking buddy from WJZ-TV, the station in Baltimore where she, Oprah, and I had worked. When she asked me to be a guest, I realized that after my appearance I would never be able to sit down and write "Rabid Nun Infects Entire Convent" again. Tabloids in general,

The Sun in particular, would be closed to me forever.

By then, it was a relief.

The music came up; Oprah looked into the camera and said, "How many times have you looked through the stories in the tabloids and for a few seconds thought to yourself, 'That could not possibly be true.'

"My next guest says chances are, no it couldn't be. He says he wrote for a national tabloid as a freelancer, says everything he wrote was fiction, found it most interesting when a picture of the people he made up would appear with the article.

"Please meet Mr. Duntoni."

She got my name wrong, even though we both worked at the same TV station in Baltimore for five years. But then, she's Oprah, and such stumbles are often overlooked in multimillionaires.

She introduced the other two people on the segment with me, Enid Sefcovic, an ex-wife of mine who also worked for *The Sun,* and Leslie Savan, who was writing a column on advertising for *The Village Voice* at the time and once served a sentence on the staff of *The National Enquirer.*

She continued, "So did you all just make it up? Did your editors say to you, 'Make it up'?"

"Yeah," I said, "it's just made up."

Laughs from the audience at my candor.

"It's fiction. It's like wrestling. As a matter of fact, it's just like wrestling."

Some people aspire to greatness. A combination of bad parenting and coming of age in Baltimore, Maryland, at the same time as John Waters pushed me in a different direction.

Only children are often left to their own devices, to their own fantasies, and often they live mostly in their heads. Add to that my parents' divorce when I was five years old, a drastically overprotective parent, and the isolation of being one of the few non-Jews in a Jewish neighborhood.

Then add the Baltimore factor. I know that other cities are toilets, but Baltimore was a special kind. And I say that in the good way.

I don't really know exactly what it was about Baltimore that spawned people like John Waters and his particular brand of inspiration. I think the chromium that leaked into the Baltimore harbor for about eighty years might have something to do with it. My theory is that the lowered IQs and other forms of brain damage that resulted in the general population stemmed from the constant exposure to chemicals like that, plus massive doses of drugs (LSD for me) helping to create warped perception and skewed reality.

Don't get me wrong, I have a spot inside me that holds feelings for Baltimore. That place might not be my heart, but it's in there someplace. Maybe my urologist found it the last time I visited him. I still have Orioles stuff all over the house, and I walk around Portland wearing my Orioles sweatshirt, cursing at Yankees fans.

But I have to say, people seem dumber in Baltimore. Most outsiders agree. I always gave that theory lip service, but when I revisited Baltimore three years after having moved to Portland, Oregon, I came to the stunning realization that I was right. People really *do* act dumber, meaner, more miserable and perverse in Baltimore than they do other places in America.

Cleveland is just as dirty and dangerous, but think about the difference between John Waters and Harvey Pekar.

Thus, it was in Baltimore and nowhere else that Divine, a three-hundred-pound transvestite, ate dog shit off a sidewalk in *Pink Flamingos* and gained worldwide acclaim.

John Waters was Baltimore's underground filmmaker in "the sixties." I was Baltimore's most visible underground journalist, writing for and later publishing the hippie paper of record there. Everybody knew each other. So I was primed to come up with these stories at some point.

Of course, John is rich and famous, and here I am hoping to sell a few of these books by doing dozens of Morning Zoo radio shows and being funny for radio "personalities" who would rather fart than talk.

But I digress.

When I mentioned to John's best friend, Pat Moran, that *The Sun* was going to buy some stories, she said, "That's John Vader's paper, isn't it?"

"Yeah! How do you know him?"

"Vader's the guy who's mentioned at the end of *Pink Flamingos*. He was the editor of *Midnight* at the time we made the picture."

"Oh, yeah! *Midnight*!"

Now I remember. In the movie, Waters made a fake *Midnight* cover with a picture of Divine and the headline "Filthiest People Alive" on it.

I was going to work for the guy who ran *Midnight*? *Midnight*? The raunchiest of the old-time tabs? He liked *my* stuff?

It was thrilling.

Enid, my ex-wife, had taken a job at *The Sun*. I was happy for her; at least she wasn't hot-walking horses at racetracks anymore. I saw my way in. Would she show a few stories to the boss? Sure she would.

I sat down at the keyboard. This came out.

GRANDMA TURNS PET DOG INSIDE OUT LOOKING FOR LOST LOTTERY TICKET by Phillip Archer

A GRANDMOTHER of four is facing a long stay in the nuthouse after she nearly turned her pet bulldog, Eddie-O, inside out.

"She thought she had hit the lottery for a couple hundred thousand dollars," said a mental health spokesperson. "But she lost the ticket and went berserk."

The woman, Ida Lee Thompson, ran through the house ripping her furniture to shreds. Huge clumps of mattress stuffing were found in her bedroom, along with what was left of her clothing, the pockets torn out. Even her padded bras were in ribbons.

Her living room suite was down to the bare wood, and in her kitchen, broken dishes and glassware were scattered all over the floor and covered by the contents of several opened cans of spaghetti sauce and oatmeal.

"She really flipped out," the spokesperson continued. "But it was what happened after she ransacked the kitchen and still couldn't find the ticket that's so bad. I've never encountered behavior like that before.

"She stuck her hand down her dog's throat and just pulled."

A neighbor heard the horrible sounds coming from the dog and called the police. When they got there, the dog was turned inside out.

The police were unable to find the woman when they battered down the door of the third-floor apartment, but after a search of the building, found her on the roof. She had taken her shirt off and was waving it around in one hand screaming, "I won the lottery! I won the lottery!" over and over.

In her other hand, police say, she was waving what was later identified as the dog's liver. A crowd, which had gathered in front of her building, began taunting her, laughing at her, and calling for her to jump off the roof. Police quickly reached her and hustled her away in a straitjacket.

As she was put into the ambulance, she screamed, "That dog! That dog! I know he's got it! Just let me at him! I know it's in there! Please, please! I won the lottery! I just can't find the ticket. I know that damned dog's got it! He ate my money! Let me at him! I won the lottery! I won the lottery!"

Neighbors said she had bought a lottery ticket every day for six years, and before that played the illegal numbers game every day for thirty years.

"She swore she was gonna hit that thing and buy everybody in the neighborhood a drink," said Karen Cox, a neighbor. "That girl bought dream books; she even went to Gypsies to get the right number. She always played 666, though. My boyfriend told her that's the devil's number. All this dog business, it looks like the work of the devil to me."

A teenaged neighbor boy told police he had seen strange rituals in her home at the time of the daily lottery drawing on TV. "The boy told us he used to spy in the windows," a police spokesperson said.

"It was pretty weird, and it usually involved the dog," he continued. "Sometimes she would take all her clothes off when the drawing came on. She would take the dog's leash and put it around her own neck, then she'd put the other end around the dog's paw like he was leading her around.

"She would get on all fours in front of the TV during the drawing and bark. When she didn't win she would go on crying jags that could last for hours. This is one messed-up lady, I'll tell you."

When asked about the dog, Cox said, "Well, she really loved that dog. I don't know what people get out of bulldogs, I think they're as ugly as sin, but old Eddie-O never left her side. I don't know how she could do such a thing to it. Stuck her hand right inside of it. My, my, my . . ."

The mystery of what happened to her lottery ticket was solved when her 16-year-old granddaughter came home and walked in on the grisly scene. She told police that the ticket was just where it always was. In an exclusive interview, she said, "Grandma always put it right here in the pantry, next to the dog food. I don't know what got into Grandma. Maybe she was possessed. Poor old Eddie-O.

"The doctors told us Grandma could come out of the hospital in about a year, but I don't know about that. It's something I'll never for-get. Eddie-O was spread out from one end of the living room to the other. My mother and me put what was left of him in a bag and took him down to the pet cemetery. Buried him with a gravestone and all. It was the least we could do for him 'cause of what Grandma did.

"We're not gonna tell Grandma about where he is when she gets out though. You never know what she'll do. We'll just tell her the pound took him away."

Doctors say the woman is still under heavy sedation and does not remember what she did. "She's the sweetest old lady, really," said one doctor. "The only problem we have with her is during the TV lottery drawing every day. She had to be restrained for the first few weeks. Now, she only sits there and barks. That shows some progress."

Her daughter has had the woman declared mentally incompetent, and has assumed power of attorney. The first thing she did was re-deem the lottery ticket and buy bottles of champagne for all the neigh-bors. The granddaughter said, "It was the least my momma could do for all the pain Grandma caused around here."

WOMAN GOES ON HIGH-FIBER DIET, EATS HER CLOTHES

2

Oh my, I thought. Have I tapped something I didn't know was in my brain?

I had just quoted a person I had just made up. It was intoxicating.

I had spent fifteen years as a journalist and broadcaster, chasing down sources, double-checking facts, getting people to open up in interviews and now . . . now I could make the people in my stories do or say anything I wanted them to.

I was too pleased with that prospect, and how funny the story was, to consider what it might mean to my mental health when I realized (at some later date) that this little tale of horror had come out of my own head. Or even to consider why.

I kept on writing that day.

WOMAN GOES ON HIGH-FIBER DIET, EATS HER CLOTHES
by Bonnie Gitz

ALL THE talk these days about how eating a high-fiber diet can make you live a longer and happier life has inspired a woman in France to take the concept a step further. Rather than eat grains, breads and cereals that contain high fiber, Ms. Brigitte LaFleur has begun eating a special diet consisting of old clothing, sheets, towels and pillowcases.

Although she was warned by her doctor and several other experts in the field that she was risking certain death by doing so, she claims she has never felt better in her life.

"I wouldn't recommend this for everybody," she said, through an interpreter, "but I love it!"

She cooks some things; others she eats raw—silk, for instance. "I've gotten quite fond of bedsheet pasta. All you have to do is spend the time to cut them up into little strips that look like real spaghetti, or if you're like me and have a husband who works in an office, better still! He takes them to work and puts them through the paper shredder.

"Then all you have to do is add a little spaghetti sauce, some grated cheese, and there you go! Delicious!

"This morning I had a lovely bolt of cheesecloth with butter and jam. Funny they call it cheesecloth because it doesn't taste like cheese at all! It's a little bit like cotton, but more tender. I got right up from the table and washed the windows. I felt so invigorated!"

For lunch, she often cooks up a facecloth. "But for those cold winter afternoons, I like a nice wool sweater soup. I've been eating soup made from one nice woolly sweater for three weeks. The dishes last a long time because they don't spoil. I have shelves of sweater soup, and purée of blouse. With my diet, all you need is a little imagination!"

Her pride and joy is her dinner menu. "I just love making a big dinner. I consider myself an elegant person. I most enjoy making meals out of my designer gowns . . . Adolfos, Balenciagas. . . . Gwyneth Paltrow has nothing on me. When she's finished with her gowns, she just leaves them in the closet. I recycle.

"My designer gowns are an integral part of my health and fitness regimen. But you must be careful not to overcook them. You must treat them with the respect they deserve. Cut them up into little squares and fry them lightly with butter, and it's a meal any hostess would be proud to serve or wear before a king. So good-looking, and so good for you."

When asked to comment on this latest fad diet, a noted nutritionist said, "This woman is a lunatic. Eating your clothing, sheets, towels, anything like that is a very dangerous thing to do. I'm not surprised her own doctor advised against it. I would advise her to stop immediately, and any of your readers who might consider this as an alternative to a safe and sane diet should also stop. I can't make this point too strongly."

Ms. LaFleur disagrees, "People tell me there are chemicals in my diet that might harm me, but just think about how many chemicals there are in any fast-food meal. It'd rather sit myself down in front of a nice bowl of muslin any day, than have to eat disgusting hamburgers in one of those dirty fast-food hangouts. Yucchh! The thought of it makes me sick!"

Another nutritionist told us, "I expect this woman will be dead within six months if she persists in these eating habits. Clothing fibers are toxic enough by themselves, but the dyes used in them are not meant to be consumed under any circumstances!

"Where do you find these people?"

What does Ms. LaFleur's husband think about all this? He's gotten used to his wife's diet choices. "This is nothing," he told us. "She once got it into her head that wood was good for her. I had to buy all new kitchen furniture after that. I came home one night and the kitchen table and all the chairs and been put up in Seal-a-Meals."

Does he partake? "Hell, no! I take all my meals out. I guess when you're married you have to take the good with the bad."

And what was Ms. LaFleur having for dinner the night we interviewed her? "You know, I've saved the bed linens we used on our honeymoon all these years. And tonight, in honor of being in your newspaper, I'm going to make a special sheet cake."

DENTURE BANDIT STEALS FALSE TEETH FROM MOUTHS OF VICTIMS

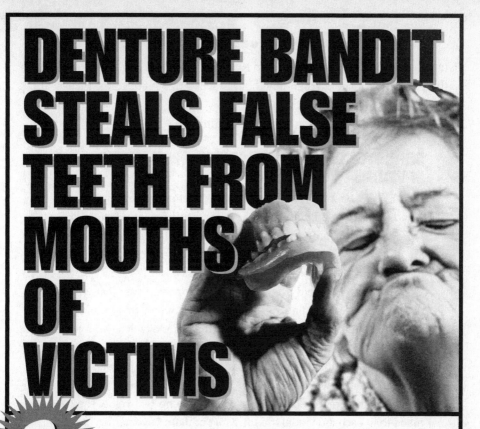

3

Yes, it's corny, I thought. Well, that's not as bad as the grandma reaching in and turning her dog inside out, certainly.

These stories could have been true, right? Maybe? What had I just written? They looked like news stories. They had the ring of authenticity to them. Of course they did; I've written hundreds of real stories, the form is ingrained. The content is where the twist comes in.

And I've seen people crazy enough to turn their dog inside out. Hell, I had been a cabdriver. I've seen people piss on fireplugs on busy street corners. I knew a guy who turned down the chance to own a troupe of real pinheads. Anything was possible, and almost anything was probable.

Although I had admired the tabs for a long time, I had never sat around trying to make up stories, but I knew I had it in me. After all, I had spent decades walking around Baltimore and watching.

Years later, whenever I would

tell somebody about having written for *The Sun*, they'd always tell me something they had made up that they thought was funny. It never is. Please stop.

I continued writing.

I began to get drunk on my own imagination.

DENTURE BANDIT STEALS FALSE TEETH FROM MOUTHS OF VICTIMS by Harrison Monroe

A THIEF has been terrorizing a six-block section of Birmingham, England, by ripping dentures out of the mouths of elderly residents. So
far, 29 men and women have had to go through the filthy terror of having a disgusting criminal put his hand in their mouths and pull their
dentures out.

Viola Johnson told *The Sun*, "My goodness, I was just walking
down the street minding my own business when this young man
came up behind me and knocked me to the ground with a two-by-four.

"I tried to scream, but when I did, he stuck his dirty hand right in
my mouth and pulled out my false teeth. Then he just ran away."

Police detectives are baffled. "We just don't know what we're
dealing with here. You know, false teeth have no real value. They are
made to fit each individual mouth. Most of them have names or serial
numbers on them. There's not exactly a black market in false teeth out
there."

The nauseating kook won't take no for an answer. Virgil Hopkins,
73, said, "I wouldn't open my mouth for nothing. He made me walk six
blocks to a garage where he threatened to pry my mouth open with a
crowbar. I just couldn't stand it no more, so I opened up and let him
take my teeth. And when he took 'em, he just ripped them out, just
ripped them out."

Police psychologists feel they are dealing with someone who's
just gone bonkers. "We don't know what he's doing with the false
teeth. Is he making some weird fetish out of them? I wonder if we're
dealing with a cult here."

The mayor has ordered security tightened around senior citizen
centers. A city hall insider told us, "The mayor is very image con-

scious. He doesn't want it getting around that this is a place where citizens are so unsafe they must fear for their own dentures."

A city councilperson is calling for the resignation of the chief of police if the monster is not caught in the next 30 days. "This has to stop! It's dentures today—what's it going to be tomorrow, glass eyes? Prosthetics? Breast implants? It's ridiculous! They know what this guy looks like. Now it's time to catch him!!"

Police have advised the elderly in the neighborhood to leave their false teeth at home when they go out, or put them in their pockets and purses. When she heard this advice, a representative of the residents' association of a local old-age home was furious. "What about when we want to go out and have a bite to eat at McDonald's, or if we want to stop and buy an apple?

"I, myself, know of a woman in our building who had just put her false teeth in and decided to go for a walk. She was pushed up against a wall by this horrible person. It took him twenty minutes of pulling to get her teeth out because of the new denture adhesives they're making nowadays. Twenty minutes he had his hand in her mouth!!

"These police better get on the stick, or we'll get some better ones, I'll tell you that!!"

The attacker, his victims report, laughs hysterically, sometimes having to stop and sit down in the middle of the attack. He has used a hammer and chisel, an electric drill, a shoehorn and a bottle opener to get the teeth.

A police officer told us, off the record, "We're up against a brick wall. What's he doing with these dentures? We've checked all the pawnshops. I don't know what people expect us to do."

But the rude thefts continue. In the latest attack, the bandit held up three people at once. The three—72, 74, and 68—were on their way home from dinner when the monster jumped out in front of them from a dark alley. He confronted them with a silver-plated ice pick and told them to cooperate or they would get hurt.

Adding a new wrinkle to his perverse methods, he forced one of the victims to remove the teeth of her 72-year-old female friend. The bandit laughed constantly as he forced the third senior citizen to watch the spectacle. The victims were made to lie atop each other and count to 700 so the sicko could run away with their dentures, which he had placed in a plastic bag.

 As soon as the police arrest this pervert, you'll be the first to read about it right here.

NEWBORN BABY SINGS LIKE ELVIS

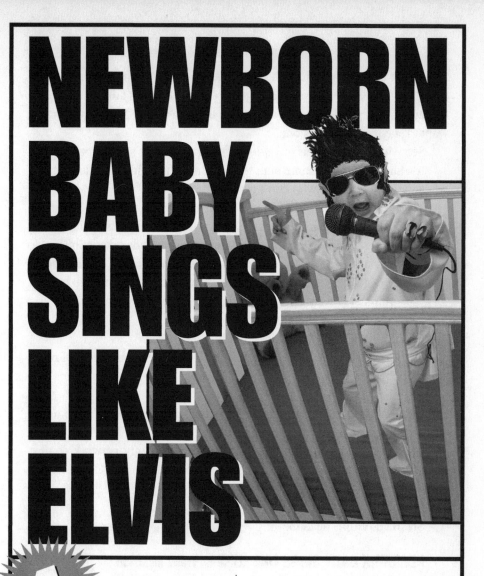

4

At the risk of offending the 22-year-old wool-hat-wearing boys who hate hippies like O'Reilly hates Franken, one of my biggest influences was the Firesign Theatre. There, I've said it, and I'm not ashamed. A recent item about them in one of those tiresome self-referential, fifteen-minute-frame-of-reference local weeklies, *The Portland Mercury,* called them an "ensemble of ex-hippies" whom the writer had seen as a high-school freshman, taken by his dad "and having not one iota of a clue as to what was going on." He recommended the show to disc jockeys and sound engineers, but ended his still-clueless item by saying, "Otherwise, if you didn't live through World War II, you might want to stay home for this one."

See what I mean? This guy *still* doesn't know what's going on.

It's hard to explain something to someone who thinks you don't get it, when they are the ones who don't get it.

The Firesign Theatre is as important in explaining, defining, satirizing, and criticizing American culture and politics (and religion) as Susan Sontag or anyone else. And they're a whole lot funnier. They did and continue to do this while creating a new paradigm of recorded performance. Their work, in fact, *is* psychedelic, in the best sense of the word. And it continues to be right up to this minute. (I went to the show the kid was writing about.)

And they make you laugh.

Without them, you wouldn't be holding this book.

So go pour some coffee, barista boy. Call me when your frame of reference gets beyond the end of your nose.

Am I being too defensive?

Okay, back to the thrilling tale of my appearance on *Oprah*. We return you now to Chicago and a TV studio full of rapt women.

I had picked out some of my favorite stories for my network confessional, and brought some of the issues of the paper with me. Oprah looked over at the monitor as they put up some of my stories.

"Here are some of the stories of yours."

She read off this headline:

NEWBORN BABY SINGS LIKE ELVIS by Frank McShann

A LIFELONG Elvis fan had her dream come true last week when she gave birth to a nine-pound baby boy who looked exactly like Elvis Presley. The baby shocked the doctors and nurses in the delivery room by beginning to sing shortly after birth.

"I know it sounds crazy," said the delivery nurse, "but we all agreed it sounded just like 'Don't Be Cruel'!"

The mother, Priscilla Gladys Pressey, had her name changed from

Bessie Womack shortly after she got pregnant. Priscilla was Elvis's wife's name. Gladys was Elvis's mother's name. Pressey wanted to use the name Presley, but the judge refused to allow it.

She might be Elvis's greatest fan. Every room of her ten-room house is covered in Elvis memorabilia, from floor to ceiling.

Her husband, Robert Womack, whom she divorced after becoming pregnant, told us that he thought she had gone off the deep end.

"I remember the night she got pregnant like it was yesterday," he said. "She made me dress up in that Elvis outfit. She had a lot of authentic Elvis clothes. Things he had worn onstage. She made me wear one of his Vegas outfits that night. You know, the white jumpsuit with the big belt buckle? And she made me put on a rubber Elvis mask, the kind that fits over your whole head.

"I know it sounds strange, but it was the best sex we ever had. She was fantastic! Unfortunately, as soon as she found out she was pregnant, she dumped me."

The result, little baby Elvis, soon became the hit of the hospital. Doctors, nurses and patients stopped by to see and hear the miracle baby. By the end of his second day of life, he had learned three songs: "All Shook Up," "Don't Be Cruel," and "Viva Las Vegas"!

Relaxing at home after her stay in the hospital, Priscilla told us that she wasn't surprised at either the birth or the singing.

"Oh, I knew it was going to happen this way. When I was first pregnant, I went to sleep with a tape recorder strapped to my stomach. I have all of Elvis's songs. I let it play all night while I slept, the whole time I was carrying him."

Later in her pregnancy, when her stomach was distended with the bulk of the child, she placed headphones on either side of it so that the unborn superstar could hear the songs in stereo.

As she talked, she held the baby in her arms. Little Elvis was wearing an outfit she had made during her pregnancy. It was a replica of the outfit Elvis wore on *The Ed Sullivan Show* in 1957. In fact, she had made 15 different outfits for the child, each a replica of a famous Elvis costume.

"I can't wait to show you what he looks like in his little black patent leather diaper and matching jacket," she said.

Even more remarkable was the fact that the baby sang a different song each time she changed his outfit.

"I love when he sings 'How Great Thou Art.' You know, he just came from heaven, so when he sings it, I feel like he really knows God.

"I can't wait for his voice to change so he can turn me on like he did the first time he was alive."

Priscilla says she feels like Jesus' mother because she knows her miracle Elvis baby will bring so much enjoyment to the world when he grows up.

Little Elvis Aaron Pressey is quite a sight because he looks so much like the dead singer. His birth hair is combed into a pompadour, but the amazing thing is that he was born with sideburns.

Priscilla has fixed up the baby's room to look like Elvis's jungle room at Graceland, his favorite. Little Elvis's crib is surrounded by jungle plants, a waterfall, lots of tiger and zebra skins, and several bodyguards.

"Just imagine how many people would love to kidnap my little boy," she said.

"It's a dream come true," says Little Elvis's new mama. "I bet every Elvis fan in the world envies me. But I'm the only one who is going to have the pleasure of watching him grow into manhood.

"If he loves me as much as Elvis loved his mom, I'll feel like I've died and gone to heaven!"

THE HUMAN TERMITE:

He's Eating the Neighborhood

5

That got laughs. Lots of laughs.

These ideas, I discover now, as I rewrite these stories, didn't come out of nowhere. Some little thing in life triggered them: standing in line behind an old lady who is buying dozens of lottery tickets; seeing fad-diet fanatics preaching in infomercials; and then there was that Elvis Presley merchandise party I did a TV story on. I am sorry to say that I didn't make up the part about the wife having the husband wear a full-head Elvis mask. I actually heard that suggestion being made by a woman who was holding what amounted to an Elvis Tupperware party. I can still see her holding up the mask, and the titters among the housewives in attendance, as though they were picturing their own husbands with it on, in bed.

I have always felt that tabloid stories are just one small jump ahead of reality. A very small jump.

Oprah read another title to the audience.

THE HUMAN TERMITE: HE'S EATING THE NEIGHBORHOOD
by **Judy Dunn**

A 55-year-old unemployed window washer is in a government mental hospital after a group of his neighbors had him committed for eating large portions of their homes.

"We didn't want to put him in jail," said one of Jack Clinton's ex-neighbors, "but he would get up at night, go outside, and eat parts of our houses. This had to stop."

Another neighbor was less charitable. Barbara Swartz told us that Clinton had done $25,000 worth of damage to her house.

"I don't think it's very funny! He's a termite! I'm going to have to take out a second mortgage to get the damage fixed. What the hell did he think he was, a beaver?"

She added that Clinton is now penniless and she can't collect a cent from him.

A solid family man for 30 years, Clinton began going haywire when he was fired from the window-washing job he had held for the past 25 years. Six months after he got fired, he began buying large quantities of lumber.

His wife left him soon after that. Susan Clinton told us that her husband stopped eating her cooking three weeks after he got fired. "He wouldn't eat anything but nuts for a while," she said. "Then he would only eat acorns. He would go gather them himself, but more and more he would bring in pieces of bark with the nuts.

"One night, in front of the TV, I saw him eating the nuts and bark, too! It just got worse after that. He began to chew on the doors. He kept telling me not to worry, that it was perfectly normal. He liked it so much, and he was taking a lot of vitamins. I just thought it was a phase.

"But when he brought in all that lumber . . . There was lumber in every room. He wouldn't go out and look for a job. He would just sit around all day, watching the soaps and eating boards."

Susan tearfully described the day she had to pack up and go. She claims that her husband ran out of lumber and began dismantling the house.

"When he ripped out the stairs to the second floor, I threw in the towel."

Over the next two months, he devoured much of the interior of his home. Apparently, the trouble with the neighbors began when Clinton tired of his own home and began eating theirs. Some of them thought they had termites. In reality, their problem was the twisted and sick mind of Jack Clinton. Repeatedly, he would sneak out of his house and nibble on five or six houses per night, taking small bites from each house, near the foundation.

It wasn't until five different termite exterminating companies showed up on Clinton's block that his neighbors began to figure out what was going on. When none of the exterminators found termites, the neighbors held a meeting to decide what to do.

"We didn't know how the hell to deal with it," said Barbara Swartz. "We had the health department, structural engineers . . . nobody could figure it out. If it wasn't for my 12-year-old's good eyes, we may have never caught him."

Swartz's son, Barry, saw a shadowy figure in the bushes next to their house and quickly turned on the porch light. He was shocked to find Clinton taking a bite out of their front steps. According to Swartz, her son ran into her bedroom and said, "Mom, Mr. Clinton is eating our house!"

When she ran outside and confronted Clinton, he ran away. Swartz called all the neighbors and told them what happened. Later that week, another neighbor spotted Clinton trying to eat his garage door. The police were called and Clinton was quickly locked up in the psycho ward.

Since then, mental health authorities have been holding him in a concrete cell until they find out how to cure him. He is fed intravenously twice a day because he still refuses to eat anything but wood. Hospital officials say they're surprised he's still alive.

"My guess is that he kept on taking vitamins the whole time. If that's true, it's his only remaining bit of sanity. We may never know what triggered this. Apparently, he got fired because he was too fat to fit on the window ledges anymore. Maybe this started as some kind of fad diet. Maybe we'll never know.

"It's hard enough for alcoholics to stay away from booze—how are you going to keep this guy away from wood? Put him in a submarine?"

GHOSTS OF ELVIS, BING, JIMI, LENNON TO APPEAR ON TV SPECIAL

6

Bigger laughs.

I had always loved eating stories. I did lots of them for TV, real ones. For three years running I did stories on Danny "Killer" Marsh, a guy on the Eastern Shore of Maryland who kept trying to break the world's record for eating raw eggs. The first year, he had gotten drunk the night before and threw up after drinking nineteen of them out of beer mugs. The second year, he had been in a car accident a week before the contest, a major factor in causing him to throw up the eggs again. The third year, a number of others joined him in the attempt. Killer threw up again, but two others beat the record. One poor soul drank/ate thirty-two, and another one, a huge guy, laughed his way to fifty before he quit.

I'm not sure what it was about Maryland. I also did a story on the man who broke the world's record for eating raw oysters. He guzzled a couple hundred of them from beer mugs, to a cheering crowd. I was seeing a sensitive young lady at the time, and I knew the relationship was doomed when she turned her head away from the screen as he poured the oysters down his throat. By the way, after he finished wiping his mouth, the guzzler said that the oysters had no effect on his sex life, record or not.

Another memorable eating story featured a guy who took a bite out of a live hard crab, right through the eyes. The station I worked for got angry letters after that aired.

I'll never forget the guy who won bar bets by eating drinking glasses. I put him in a TV story, too. Bloody mouth and all.

Oprah read the next story headline.

GHOSTS OF ELVIS, BING, JIMI, LENNON TO APPEAR ON TV SPECIAL by Frank McShann

FAMED GHOST hunter Joachim Kutchmer claims, in a media release, that he has gotten the ghosts of four famous popular musicians on videotape and will sell the show to the highest bidder.

He claims that Elvis Presley, Bing Crosby, Jimi Hendrix and John Lennon are seen performing songs written after their deaths. "Nobody would believe me if Elvis walked out and did 'Don't Be Cruel,' would they? Elvis sings 'Born in the U.S.A.,' the Bruce Springsteen song, which was written long after Elvis died.

"He also participates in the quartet. They all sing together! I guarantee it's gonna knock your socks off!"

According to Kutchmer, Bing Crosby sings two of his big hits— "When the Blue of the Night Meets the Gold of the Day" and "White Christmas"—and "Hello," the Lionel Richie tune.

Jimi Hendrix does "The Wind Cries Mary," "Purple Haze" and "Purple Rain," the title tune from Prince's movie.

"That one, boy oh boy . . . it's the best," said Kutchmer. "I know my field is parapsychology, but I think Jimi Hendrix sings 'Purple Rain' better than Prince does. He rocks!"

John Lennon sings "Imagine," "Yellow Submarine" and "Valotte," a hit by his son Julian.

"You know, people think of parapsychologists as stuffy old men," the 66-year-old Ph.D. continued, "or Gypsies with violins playing in the background, but all the ghost hunters I know are rock-and-rollers. When we contact our spirit guides, we always ask about performers we have listened to and loved.

"One guide told me he had seen a kind of 'Woodstock' in the netherworld. All the dead stars were there. My spirit guide said he had a blast. I told him I wished I could have been there, although I wasn't quite ready to die," Kutchmer said, laughing. "But then I said I would give almost anything to hear them play together. The spirit told me he might be able to arrange something."

Kutchmer said that the next time he convened a séance in his Berlin apartment, he listened to a lot of music beforehand and was prepared for anything. "My spirit guide was the first to appear, in the vacant chair we always leave for him. He told me my soul was particularly alive that night, and that it was bouncing all over the universe. He asked what we wanted to do.

"I spoke right up and said I wanted to hear from Elvis. The spirit replied, laughingly, 'All right, you deserve this. You've been doing so much good in the world, we're going to give you a treat. Meet the king himself, Elvis Presley!!' "

The parapsychologist told us that Elvis entered the room through the speakers on his sound system. "There he was—it was really Elvis! He launched right in, did four songs, said, 'Thank you very much,' and then disappeared. The spirit guide told us that Elvis had left the building."

Two months later, the spirit guide brought Jimi Hendrix, and then John Lennon. The following day, Kutchmer's mother, dying of cancer, asked her son if the spirit guide might be able to bring back Bing Crosby, her favorite.

A month went by, and one night when Kutchmer was in his mother's hospital room, the old crooner seeped into the room through a bedside radio. Der Bingle was in fine voice and was very nice to the woman, displaying none of the nastiness and violence that had been attributed to him after his death.

Before he left, Bing said a little prayer and promised to sing for her when they met in the afterlife.

The ghost hunter would not reveal how he got all of them to appear on videotape, but he said that it was easier than shooting a real TV show. "Well, you know, they have the power to appear on anybody's VCR through the cable connection. When I talked to the spirit guide about raising millions of dollars for Ethiopian famine relief by having the dead stars do a TV special, he said, 'Boy, that's a tough one. I'm going to have to take that up with the big guy himself.'

"We didn't hear any more about it until one day I came home and found that my VCR had been tampered with. When I pushed Play, instead of *Jane Fonda's Workout,* I found this marvelous TV special starring Elvis, Jimi, Bing and John."

When pressed on their quartet performances at the end of the show, Kutchmer said, "It's so cute, you'll just die! Oh. I didn't mean that literally."

In the finale of the tape, Elvis, Jimi, Bing and John do their own version of "Ghostbusters."

DEAD DAUGHTER LEAVES MESSAGE OF LOVE ON DADDY'S VCR

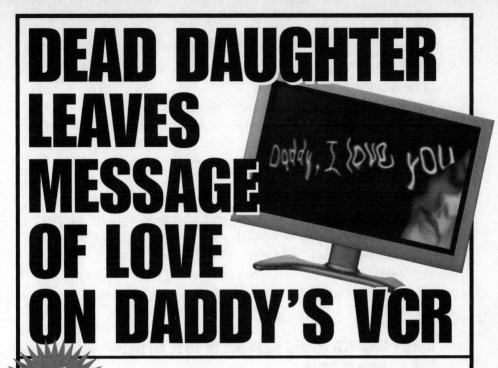

Daddy, I love you

7

Big laughs. Applause. Oprah looked at me like a Sunday-school teacher and said, "So Tom, when you were doing this, did you think you were doing something that was immoral?"

"I was writing fiction."

"And you knew it?"

"Everybody knew it," I answered, not understanding exactly how I could not know I was making something up.

But let's get back to the long road of growing dread that led to my sitting in front of Ms. Winfrey.

I sent my first stories to the paper, and a week later the ex called to tell me how well they'd been received, that *The Sun* wanted to buy them, and that they wanted more. Call this number and ask for Blah Blah.

It wasn't Vader's number. Not yet. It was a pleasant lady who told me I would be getting $25 per story.

Huh?

Twenty-five dollars? That's all?

Yeah, that's what we pay.

They were *that* cheap. I had always heard there were big bucks to be made in the tabs. These were not big bucks. And it wasn't till a couple months later that they told me (inadvertently) that if they used the title in the teasers on the cover I would make an additional $10. If they used it as the banner headline that week, I would get an additional $25.

So if I hit the jackpot I could make as much as $50 a story.

I said to Vader one time, "What about the big money I always heard people made writing for the tabs?"

"Oh, yeah, but that's at the *Enquirer,* or our other paper, *The Globe.*"

"Can I write for *The Globe*?"

"You could, Tom, but those stories have to have some truth to them."

"Oh," I said, disappointed, "I'm not sure I want to do that." By that time I had become addicted to my own imagination. I didn't care how much more I could make. As long as I could write "Dead Daughter Leaves Message of Love on Daddy's VCR" and find, when I opened the paper to my story, pictures of the two people I had made up staring at me from the page. It was oh so seductive.

DEAD DAUGHTER LEAVES MESSAGE OF LOVE ON DADDY'S VCR by Simon McAvand

"MOMMY AND I are happy and living in heaven, Daddy," said the fuzzy picture on the TV screen. It was Teddy Gooden's little girl, Candi. She had been dead for two years, but here she was talking to her father from his VCR.

Little Candi was speaking to her daddy from heaven.

Ted Gooden had worked nights since the deaths, at the hands of a brutal murderer, of his wife, Ann, 33, and their daughter, Candi, 8. He couldn't sleep more than a couple of hours at a time because of the horrible nightmares. They were always the same—the torture and killing of his family, the unspeakable things the killer made his wife and child do before he butchered them.

Ted had set his VCR to record "Family Ties" while he was at work. When he came home, he found the tape had recorded all the way to the end. He thought there was something wrong with it. He watched the show for about 15 minutes until he dozed off.

"It was another slow-motion replay of the murders. It always slows down when he swings the ax and cuts off Ann's . . ." Gooden broke down, crying, for the first of several times during the interview. Ann had been killed by decapitation.

"All of a sudden I was being awakened by my daughter's voice calling me. I guess I thought I was still dreaming, but I opened my eyes and saw her on the TV screen. She was beautiful again, nothing like what I had to identify for the coroner. There hadn't been hardly enough to make out then, but here she was all pretty, with a new dress on, and had her hair fixed real nice. She was whole again.

"And she was saying, 'Daddy, Daddy, Daddy, aren't you proud of me? Look, Daddy, I'm on TV!' "

Gooden leaped from his chair and saw that the VCR was still running, but instead of little Jennifer and Justin in the sitcom, he saw a cloudy image of his own daughter. Panicked and unable to think clearly, as you might expect, Gooden pushed the Stop button on the remote. The image of his daughter disappeared. He pushed the Play button; the tape engaged and the same image of his daughter appeared on the screen.

"I just sat down and watched my little dead daughter talk to me," Gooden said. "She spoke so sweetly, saying, 'Mommy and I know how unhappy you have been all these years since we went away, and we don't want you to feel bad. We miss you and we know you miss us, but we're doing fine, Daddy. Do you like my dress? Mommy did my hair for me.' "

Gooden broke down again, at this point, during our interview. When he was able to continue, he said, "Then she talked some more to me about how she and Ann were allowed earthly visits every few years, and that Ann wanted me to see Candi so that my mind might be able to be a little more at rest.

"But it isn't at rest. Since I watched the tape, and I've watched it a hundred times, I want to die and go to heaven so I can be with them. But I know I can't, because suicide is a sin, and I'll burn in hell if I kill myself."

Psychic experts have been predicting this phenomenon for a long time. Raymond Baylis, one of the leading experts in the field of recording the voices of the dead, wrote as early as 1982 that with the invention of new technologies, "Ghosts could use the medium of television, telephones, or computers."

Gooden refuses to allow experts to view the tape. In fact, the only person who has seen it, other than Gooden, is the manager of his apartment building, who was sworn to secrecy. She told us, "Look, I can't say anything about it, but you don't see me running around calling Teddy a liar, do you?

"I will say it is the best, most amazing TV show I've ever seen."

Gooden said, "You're the only newspaper I've told. I don't think anybody else would believe me. But I know your readers are good people, God-fearing people and God-loving. I know they'll believe my story. I don't know if this has happened to anybody else, but if it has, please write to me. Maybe then I'll release the tape."

When pressed to reveal the details of his family's life in heaven, Gooden said, "She didn't go into detail. She just said it was, well, heavenly. I remember she said, 'Oh, Daddy, Mommy and I have so much fun all the time and we've been planning this surprise for you for so very long because we both love you.' "

Gooden continued, "She told me that the next time they're allowed an earthly visit, my wife would be the one to come, but she didn't tell me when it would be. So every night I set my VCR the same way I did the night my precious Candi visited me. I keep waiting every night, every night . . ." Gooden began sobbing uncontrollably at this point.

Later, after he had regained his composure, he told us that either he or his apartment manager has the tape in their possession at all times. He did not bring it with him to the interview.

"It has changed my life, I'll tell you, because the last thing she said on the tape was a message from Ann. It was to tell me not to grieve anymore. To go out and find a nice girl to love, and that it was bad for me to be like I was. That she felt it was her fault that I was like that, her dying and all.

"So I did it, but we never go to my place because I never know when Ann will show up on my VCR, and I don't want to be there with another woman when she does.

"You know, my precious little Candi pulled me through. My sweet little girl. It's everything knowing she's safe and happy with the Lord."

If any of our readers have had similar experiences, please send them to us.

READERS SEND IN EVIDENCE OF GHOSTS ON THEIR VCRs—
FROM MURDERERS TO MOTHERS-IN-LAW

8

Little did I know that recording the voices of the dead would be the premise of a major motion picture years later. Nor did I know that years after I wrote this there would be a worldwide cult of people who make their living convincing people that they can record the voices of the dead. I even interviewed some of them later on. One played a recording of what he said was a dead person saying, "It's much tooooo coooooolllld in heeerrrre." Well, why not? Hey didn't you see it in *The Sun* before? Must be true if it's in the newspaper, right?

In some ways, my dead daughter story is sicker than my gross-out stories. How did that come out of me? What is this stuff saying about me? That was the first time this question had crossed my mind. But I was in deep by now, and since sequels are the essence of entertainment—and if I had become this shameless—why not floor it and keep going? When *The Sun*'s editor accepted the dead daughter story, I knew there was a Part Two in it for me. I had asked for letters, hadn't I? I might as well make them up.

READERS SEND IN EVIDENCE OF GHOSTS ON THEIR VCRS— FROM MURDERERS TO MOTHERS-IN-LAW by Simon McAvand

WE RECENTLY published the story of Teddy Gooden, who received a message on his VCR from his dead daughter, Candi. She and her mother had been brutally slashed to death by a madman with a butcher knife. One night, long after the murders, Candi appeared on her daddy's VCR, reassuring him that she and her mommy were well and living in heaven.

At the time we ran the story, we asked our readers to write in and tell us if anything similar had happened to them. Judging by the responses we have received, communication through VCRs is fast replacing psychic mediums as the favorite means for those who have passed over to the other side to reach the world of the living.

The responses vary greatly, from nagging mothers-in-law, to presidential campaign speeches, to confessions from murderers. Here are some samples. In order to protect the privacy of the letter writers, we have not included the locations of the occurrences.

MRS. RHONDA GETTIER   I was so happy to read about Teddy Gooden and his little daughter, Candi. A similar thing happened to me and my VCR, but I thought I was crazy. I wouldn't even tell my therapist about it. Then, when I saw your story, I was so relieved.

My husband's mother had been a constant source of irritation in my life while she was alive. Every day she would call me up and nag me. What did her little boy have for breakfast? Did I pack him a lunch? What was he going to eat for dinner? Did he wear his gloves to work?

And when it came to sex, I guess she thought he was going to be with her forever, because she would call up just about the time he and I would be getting it on. She knew it and she just wanted to stop it.

Just like clockwork, she would call and he would quit. So when she died, I was relieved.

Imagine how upset I was when I came home from work the other day and found her fat face on a tape in my VCR. I always set it up so I can record my stories when I am at work. I sat down and watched "One Life to Live," and when that was over, I was expecting to watch "General Hospital" before I had to start dinner.

All of a sudden, instead of the program, there she was, my dead mother-in-law, standing there with her hands on her hips, looking straight at me from the TV screen and saying, "All right, bitch! Thought you got rid of me, didn't you? I'll give you fair warning: if you don't take care of my boy to my liking, you can expect to hear a lot more from me! Understand?"

Then "General Hospital" came back on. I was frantic, but then I saw your article on Teddy and Candi. Now I have taken steps to ensure that I never see her again. I burned the tape and spilled a hot cup of coffee into the VCR so it doesn't work anymore. My husband doesn't care; we only got it so I could record my stories.

I never told him. I hope I've gotten rid of her again, for good!

ROBERT GLYNDON   This happened to me and several of my neighbors. I bowl every Monday night, and me and my buddies don't get a chance to see "Monday Night Football," so we all record it on our VCRs while we're bowling. We watch the game when we get home so we can all talk about it at work the next day.

I got home and sat down to watch. In the middle of the second quarter, the game switched off and Lyndon Johnson came on the screen. You know, the guy who used to be president? He was wearing a tuxedo and was talking about how he ought to be president. I thought something had gone wrong with my VCR, but when I went to work, all the guys from the bowling team said they had seen the same thing. All except for Charlie who lives next door. He watched the game live because he hurt his foot and couldn't bowl. He said he watched the whole game and never saw Lyndon Johnson.

We called up the cable company, and they said they didn't run the speech, and they said nobody else had either, not even the network. The strange thing was that Johnson mentioned all of our names, all of us on the bowling team.

He said, "And I want to talk to you, Bob Glyndon." And then he named the others, all of them. I don't know why he wanted to single us out.

I showed the tape to a political science teacher who lives on my block and he identified Hubert Humphrey, and way in the back, President Eisenhower, Winston Churchill and Joseph Stalin. I was baffled until I saw your article about the dead daughter.

Funny thing is, he told us to vote against Bush!

FRED AND SUSAN FADER You asked for VCR incidents involving ghosts. We had a murderer confess on ours. We had moved into our house last year, it had been abandoned for several years. We didn't know why. One night we had gone out to dinner and left the VCR on to record the rest of the news so we could watch it later. Instead of the news, we found a gruesome sight. We thought it was a horror movie, but it was real.

It was a severed head that talked! It said, "Forgive me, forgive me! I have been punished enough! I didn't want to kill you. I don't know why I did. Now I'm forced to spend eternity as a severed head! Please forgive me! Please forgive me!" And then it disappeared.

We did some digging in local papers and found that a couple of years before we moved to town a man had killed his wife and two children. He was trying to escape when he ran into the back of a semi in his car at 85. They found his head a quarter mile away, and the rest of him still in the car, pinned under the truck with his seat belt still buckled.

They had run a picture of him next to the article and it was the same guy who had been on our VCR. What do you think of that?

Keep Sending Your Messages from Beyond!

NEW GENETIC DISCOVERY CAN MAKE YOUR DOG SMELL LIKE A PIZZA

and CLOWN GHOSTS SAVE DYING BOY

9

"Where do these stories come from?" Oprah asked me.

"A sick mind," I answered.

By the time I did *Oprah,* I knew how sick I could be.

For every cute story I wrote, like

"New Genetic Discovery Can Make Your Dog Smell Like a Pizza," and every heartwarming story, like "Clown Ghosts Save Dying Boy," there was one that the devil made me write, like "Man Sells Human Bodies from Chemical Disaster to Starving Ethiopians as Meat."

NEW GENETIC DISCOVERY CAN MAKE YOUR DOG SMELL LIKE A PIZZA by Steve Devlin

AN AUSTRALIAN geneticist has developed a process that will soon be available in the United States: an injection given to pregnant dogs and cats that can make the newborn puppy or kitten come out smelling like a rose, a pine forest, expensive perfume, a marijuana cigarette, or one of several kinds of foods, including pizza.

The process involves splicing the genes from these substances with the genes your little poochie or kitty already carries, and passes along to her offspring.

"It all came up quite by accident," according to Dr. Ralph D. Colbert of Perth, Australia. "I'd been working on the concept of making various fragrances for a perfume company. I had developed a new process using genetics. It's too complicated for your readers, but let's just say that if you cut one gene in half, the other half of the gene retains certain properties. If you take the correct side of it, you get the smell.

"I was working on scented underwear. My boss said he could sell millions of panties if they smelled like, say, flowers, for instance. So I went right to work on it, especially since he promised me ten percent.

"Well, six months later, I stumbled onto the secret."

When asked to reveal the secret, Colbert laughed and said, "Ha! I'd have to be a fool. What do you take me for? I'm sitting on a gold mine here!"

Colbert was working late in his lab and his first batch of rose-scented panties was ready. The problem had been in getting the smell to last. This batch had been in storage for two months. In addition, Colbert's lovely assistant, Molly, had been instructed to wear the same pair of scented panties for the same two months. She wasn't allowed to change them or wash them, even during her menstrual period.

"It was quite an occasion," said Colbert. "I had taken one of the panties out of the batch we had stored and put it on the lab table. Then I asked Molly to take off her pair and place it next to the fresh one. She didn't hesitate. She didn't even leave the room. She was very much intrigued by my research.

"I picked up the fresh panty and sniffed it. Ahhh . . . the scent of a beautiful red rose. Then I picked up Molly's. I tell you, I was almost afraid to try it. But when I did, they smelled just like the fresh one. We all hugged and kissed each other, because we had discovered a long-lasting replication of a wonderful scent, the rose.

"My goodness, we broke open the champagne and got quite drunk in celebration. We scientists are supposed to be stuffy old men, but we're not—we have a sense of humor, too, especially after three bottles of French champagne. We were all laughing it up and I said, only as a joke, mind you, what if we injected a little of our artificial pizza scent into the pregnant cat we kept around the lab?

"Molly grabbed the creature; I got the syringe ready and injected the cat. Three months later, I walked into the lab and noticed the odor of pizza. It smelled just like our pizza scent, but I didn't know where it was coming from.

"I looked over in the corner and there was our lab cat with four brand-new kittens. I picked one up and, sure enough, it smelled just like a pizza pie!"

Since then, Colbert has found a market for his discovery. "The panties are really selling well, but the animal scent business has taken off. Veterinarians all over the world have been ordering our product.

"One satisfied customer, a woman from Texas, who refused to give her name, told us, 'When the puppies were born, I kept the one that smelled like cinnamon. I told my husband I didn't want no more of that dog smell in my house. Yuchh! I hate it! But now when my black Lab walks around, it's like having a living cookie in my house. The only thing I'd like is if they could do something about the smell when they go to the bathroom."

Colbert is working on that. "It presents a totally different problem. We have to work with the genes that determine digestive system function, but I feel confident that within a year or two, we'll have cat boxes smelling like anything except you-know-what."

Animal rights groups in Australia don't like Colbert's discovery. Mavis Quarterberg, a spokesperson, said there are a number of things to think about. "First of all, we're doing research to find out what this does to the relationship between mother and offspring. We're not so sure the mother will want to feed a kitten that smells like jambalaya. I mean, suppose a human baby was born and it smelled like cat food? Would the mother want to care for it as much?

"And another thing—who's to say some madman can't take this discovery and inject a pregnant woman with it? Imagine the poor child having to walk about for the rest of his life smelling like Italian food. We're taking steps to put Dr. Colbert and his bunch right out of business!"

Unconfirmed reports say that the potential exists for dogs to want to eat other dogs and cats because of the pizza fragrance.

But Colbert discounts all criticism. "Dogs don't even like pizza. There were groups like hers when the Pasteurs were making their discoveries. There were people who said the earth was flat and Columbus was going sail off the edge, too.

"We're confident that this is the wave of the future. After all, everybody loves their pets, but nobody wants that awful doggy smell in their house, not to mention the litter box.

"The next big thing for us is going to be flavors. We're working with a local cattlemen's association to breed barbecue flavor right into the beef. When that happens, our only limitations will be those of our own imaginations."

CLOWN GHOSTS SAVE DYING BOY by Simon McAvand

AN EIGHT-year-old cancer victim told hospital officials he was visited by the ghosts of circus clowns. Tommie Norman of Birmingham, England, told officials at Covington Hospital that he had been awakened in the middle of the night by a half-dozen circus clowns who performed for him for an hour before disappearing.

At first, hospital officials were skeptical of the boy's story. Says public relations representative William McCleod, "I know what you're going to say, this is just the dreaming of an eight-year-old. That's what we thought, too, until we conducted an investigation.

"Of course, the first thing we did was to suggest to Tommie that he had just been dreaming. But he's a smart little kid, and he told me he knew the difference between dreaming and not dreaming. I didn't press the issue with him because he was so happy; happier than I had seen him since he was admitted. It was really the first time I had ever seen him smile."

McCleod took reports from all nurses on duty that night, and none of them reported hearing anything out of the ordinary. It wasn't until three days later that the nurses began to realize that they had all dozed off that night.

"It was odd," said Patricia O'Sullivan, the nurse in charge that night. "You know, when nurses have to work nights, sometimes if everything is quiet and everybody is okay, we doze off. It doesn't happen every night, but once in a while it does.

"We're all amazed at how much little Tommie has improved since his clown dream."

One of the other nurses said, "I thought I had fallen asleep, too. All the nurses thought they had. We all tried to remember when it was, and it was really weird but we all thought it had been around 2:30 A.M. It was like some force put us all to sleep at the same time."

Hospital officials began to delve into the case a little more deeply after that. They tape-recorded a conversation between nurse O'Sullivan and Tommie. Always eager to talk about his clown visit, Tommie explained his experience in great detail. The hospital allowed us to reprint portions of the transcript:

NURSE: So you were just sleeping when your little friends came in? Did they wake you up?
TOMMIE: Well, Miss Pat, you know how much I hurt all the time then?
NURSE: Yes, it was real bad, wasn't it?
TOMMIE: Yeah, real bad. Well, I kept waking up and going to sleep. I think I was awake, though, when they came in, but I don't know. I know what they did when they were here, though.
NURSE: What's the first thing you remember that they did?

TOMMIE: Miss Pat, I couldn't see anything because the lights were out, and then all of a sudden there was this pink light. And when it went on I could see a whole bunch of funny people like clowns I saw in the circus last year, when my daddy took me.

NURSE: Did they talk to you?

TOMMIE: One of the clowns said, "Hi, Tommie. You can call me Bozo." He was almost as little as me. He said, "Want to see Popeye the Sailor Man?" I said, "Sure I do!"

So he turned around three times, and made himself into a regular-looking man. Then he squinched up his face and put a pipe in his mouth and turned himself into Popeye the Sailor Man.

NURSE: When you say, "turned around three times and made himself into a regular guy," you mean he changed into something else? Just like that? In front of you?

TOMMIE: Yes, Miss Pat. And his clothes changed and everything, even his funny nose. And then he did it again after Popeye, and changed himself back into Bozo.

NURSE: That's real good, Tommie. Did you reach out and touch any of them?

TOMMIE: No. I wanted to get up and play with them, but I was too sick. I wish I coulda touched them, and got up and played with them. They made me laugh so much!

NURSE: It's fun to think about, isn't it?

TOMMIE: It sure is, Miss Pat.

NURSE: What happened after Bozo showed you Popeye?

TOMMIE: Then the next clown did a trick. He pulled flowers out of the top of his head! (*Laughing*) He was so funny!!!

NURSE: (*laughing along*) It sure sounds funny.

The hospital administration is not saying that Tommie's visit was not a dream. What they do say is that Tommie's leukemia was been in remission since his experience.

"Oh, it's amazing. We're thrilled. We all like little Tommie so much, and for a while there it looked for sure that we were going to lose him.

I don't know what happened in his room that night. I couldn't even speculate. All I know is that he has had a complete turnaround. If he continues to improve, he'll be out of here in three months."

What hospital administrators won't tell you is that there is an amazing piece of evidence. During Nurse O'Sullivan's conversation with Tommie, he produced a piece of paper with a prayer written on it. Tommie said that Bozo had left it with him, and told him to pray the prayer every night before he went to sleep. If he did that, he would be protected. She read it aloud for us:

> *"O, Lord, help me to ease the strains of life for my fellow man.*
> *Help me take upon myself the pain and suffering of all others.*
> *Help me to demonstrate the kindness that links all hearts.*
> *And help me bring smiles of happiness wherever I go."*

We took the prayer to a noted circus historian, who told us that he had heard of one like it, written by an old-time clown named Bozo, the original Bozo, who had been dead for 30 years.

Perhaps nobody will solve the mystery of the clowns in Tommie Norman's hospital room. Was it a dream? Or was it a case of a healing hand from beyond?

The bottom line is that little Tommie is getting better. He even talks about becoming a clown, and indeed, since his experience, he has become the life of his hospital floor.

It's a very strange case, with a very happy ending.

MAN SELLS HUMAN BODIES FROM CHEMICAL DISASTER TO STARVING ETHIOPIANS AS MEAT FOR PREPARED MEALS

10

It helped to use current events in these things. Thousands of people were killed in a poison gas leak at a Union Carbide pesticide factory in Bhopal, India, in 1984. There were shots of the dead all over the news. At the same time, thousands were dying from starvation in Ethiopia. You remember the skin and bones, don't you?

Do you think I'm nuts for using these atrocities to inspire me to write this? Come on, what better material for jokes than horrible tragedy? Beginning to see how crazy I was getting?

Part of me is ashamed of the following story. Part of me isn't. That part is going to burn in hell.

MAN SELLS HUMAN BODIES FROM CHEMICAL DISASTER TO STARVING ETHIOPIANS AS MEAT FOR PREPARED MEALS

by **Roberta Gardner**

COMBINED FORCES of Indian and Ethiopian police departments are after a man whom they accuse of selling the bodies of the victims of the Bhopal chemical disaster to Ethiopian famine relief agencies, as meat to feed the starving people of that country.

Sava Pujira, a purveyor of gourmet meats and poultry in Rajad, a town fifty miles south of Bhopal, seemed to be doing the famine relief effort a favor by selling six tons of meat to one of the agencies providing food to the starving population of Ethiopia. He charged them half a cent per pound for the meat, claiming it was surplus mutton.

When the meat got to the refugee camps in northern Africa, it was quickly eaten by some of the starving, but those who ate it became violently ill and began to die. The meat was analyzed and was found to contain traces of methyl isocyanate, the chemical that killed more than 2,500 people in India.

The president of the famine relief agency called Pujira in India. He found that the phone had been disconnected. When he reported the incident to the Indian police, they found Pujira's business closed, his house sold and not a trace of the man anywhere.

When asked to explain how this could happen, local Indian officials told us, "It was mass pandemonium when the disaster hit. These people are the poorest of the poor. We have no real records of how many people lived in the village near the chemical plant.

"It is entirely possible that he could have come in during the worst of it, picked up 100, 200, 300 bodies, taken them to his slaughterhouse, and made hamburger out of them.

"He could have done it. Easily!"

Eyewitnesses say they saw a group of men wearing gas masks, piling up bodies on a truck the morning after the tragedy in Bhopal. They thought the men were from the local health department and were gathering up the bodies for mass burial.

But, in a twist, a spokesperson for one of the famine relief agencies denies that any of this occurred. Diane West claims the story is a rumor spread by political dissidents in order to hamper aid to the starving. "Nothing like this ever happened," she said. "I don't know where these things get started. Yes, we had an increase in deaths two weeks ago. And yes, we have received some contaminated food supplies in the past, but somebody has put a bee in your bonnet. It just isn't true."

Still, reports persist. A search of Pujira's slaughterhouse turned up human bones buried ten feet under the floor, and traces of human hair have been found in his meat-grinding machinery. This doesn't prove the case against Pujira, but it does raise speculation that he had been using human bodies all along in his gourmet meat business.

A chef in one of New Delhi's poshest restaurants told us that Pujira's meats were favorites of the richest families in his cosmopolitan city. "We had to pay a little more for his wares, but he always came up with the most exotic of the exotic. We bought penguin from him, seal and rare meats from America such as prairie dog, muskrat and mink.

"At least, that's what we thought we were buying. With what you tell me about this Ethiopian deal . . . well, we won't let it get around that we used his meats, will we?"

Because of the vast number of people dying in Ethiopian camps, it is impossible to perform autopsies. The dead are hurled into mass graves and forgotten. Therefore, it is difficult to prove the chemical poisoning charges. One scientist, Ahmad Abdullah, assigned to the camps, claims he tested tissue from two corpses and found traces of methyl isocyanate.

"Where else could it come from?" he asked. "We have no Union Carbide factories in Ethiopia. I wish we did—it would bring money into our economy—but the fact is that there is no methyl isocyanate in Ethiopia. It is not manufactured here. It is not used here."

There is no way of knowing who is right and who is wrong at the moment. Some suggest that the Indian authorities manufactured this incident in order to draw attention away from the fact that they allowed the chemical plant to run unsafely. Others say that is it just a way to make the rest of the world respond more quickly to the African starvation problem.

Still others speculate that environmentalists have stirred up all of this so that they can get the manufacture of methyl isocyanate banned from the face of the earth.

Police, continuing to search for Sava Pujira, claim the story is true. They say he is a mass murderer, and that he did, in fact, sell the ground-up flesh of contaminated victims. They promise to inform us as soon as an arrest is made.

CULT USES HUMAN HEADS FOR BOWLING BALLS

I was going to include "Cult Uses Human Heads for Bowling Balls," but something happened to me when I was rewriting the last story, a few minutes ago. I started to get that feeling again. That bad feeling. The one I used to get when I first wrote these things. The dread of my own mind. The tightness in the neck muscles. The pall that envelops me. The horror. The horror.

I'm not kidding.

I feel it.

See what I'll do for money? Maybe I should learn to push these feelings aside, like prostitutes do when they work. But how do I not think about something I'm writing? It's like your mother telling you not to think about sex when you're fifteen. Please call me if you figure that one out. On second thought, don't call me.

It must be something in me that says, "You piece of shit. How can you write that crap? Didn't your mother teach you better? You make fun of dying people, the handicapped, retards. One day you're going to end up as pathetic as they are, and then you'll remember what you've done, you rotten asshole."

If I believed in karma or destiny, I would blame my imagination for the fact that I ended up driving a cab for two years, after having had a fairly successful TV career, or for all the women who dumped me.

Lucky for me, all I believe in is my own stupidity and that my wife loves me.

So I don't really want to rewrite this story about using human heads as bowling balls, but, what the hell, you might as well see it. I mean, I wrote it.

CULT USES HUMAN HEADS FOR BOWLING BALLS by Judy Dunn

DESCENDANTS OF British religious fanatics, now living on a small island in the Caribbean Sea, have been discovered by an expedition of a private coast guard battalion. When they were discovered, they were playing in their luxurious bowling alleys inside their fabulously opulent mansion.

But they weren't using bowling balls; they were using human heads instead.

"Satan's Doctors," as they call themselves, are known to only a few people in the world. They are what's left of a fiendish sadistic religious cult that was banished from its homeland in 1886. They had taken over an entire county in the north of England, and on orders from their leader, the notorious Dr. Ralph Hastings, had enslaved much of the population there.

Hastings was a mad doctor who had hypnotized his followers into believing that he could personally talk with God. Like the followers of televangelists, they did whatever he asked them to do. They carried out gruesome medical experiments at his evil bidding.

They were thrown out of Britain when it was discovered that Hastings had his people amputate the right arms of all the adults in one village and sew them back on the wrong person, at random. This meant that a burly, muscular man might have to walk around with the right arm of a pretty 20-year-old girl for the rest of his life.

When the Home Office, in London, heard about the atrocities being committed in the name of God in Hastings's county, a party of soldiers was sent and Hastings and his followers were jailed, later to be exiled from the British Isles entirely. Even though Hastings was a nut, he was also a good politician. He had information on some of the top cabinet members. Government officials had frequented Hastings's clandestine torture salons, where Hastings's female followers performed brutal acts upon them for small fortunes in money and jewelry.

When Hastings told the Prime Minister about the conduct of his Chancellor of the Exchequer, and the unspeakable acts he had begged for, Hastings was given a small island in the remotest part of the Caribbean. He and his followers boarded a ship five days later.

They named themselves Satan's Doctors, and built a huge mansion with the materials they had brought with them. They also found a tribe of people living nearby, and began to use them in Hastings's cruel, twisted medical experiments.

Last year, the Caribbean Coastal Service boat pulled into the camouflaged dock at the island, looking for drug smugglers, but what these battle-hardened men found affected them so profoundly that when the expedition was over, they were all granted psychological discharges.

Guarding the dock was a grotesque monster, a dwarf with his head sewn on backwards. When he saw the Coastal Service officers with their rifles drawn, the dwarf began running backwards toward the mansion.

The commander of the soldiers called a halt, as he and his 15 men stood transfixed by the sight of a dwarf forced to run backwards because his head had been sewn on that way. You see, if he ran forwards, he wouldn't be able to see where he was going. This was one of Satan's Doctors' little jokes.

Wait, wait. Hold on here for a minute. As I was rewriting that, it all came back to me even more strongly than before: This sucks. Anybody got any Xanax?

Do you think rogue regimes, which torture and maim, employ guys like me to think up horrible things to do to their opponents? Does W?

And then I think: These things came out of *me,* straight from my brain, out of nowhere. And now I have to relive the process. You have to understand, I haven't read these stories, in their entirety, for a long time. Over the years, just the headlines were enough to make the girls laugh.

I had forgotten about the dwarf.

Jesus.

I hope you know what a sacrifice I'm making for your pathetic entertainment.

Here's the rest.

When the soldiers burst into the recreation building, they found a horrifying sight—what looked like normal bowling gone berserk. As they got closer, they saw that one of the bowlers had his fingers inside the eyes, nose and mouth of a human skull.

Another man had his fingers inside the eyes, nose and mouth of a freshly severed human head and was preparing to try to pick up a spare.

On the ball rack, awaiting use by other bowlers, were six more human heads, some skulls, some freshly severed, some in a putrid state of decay. And in the ball-cleaning machine was the disgusting sight of a human head spinning around and around.

One of the bowlers approached the commander and identified himself as Sir John Hastings, "King of the Island." A soldier who broke a military-enforced gag order to give us an interview said, "He asked if we were pirates. Our commander said no, and explained who we were.

"Hastings got very angry and told the commander he was trespassing. He said the island belonged to him, that it had been given to his grandfather by the King of England.

"He said he would allow us safe passage off the island, but that if we ever came back, we would all be killed, no matter how well armed we were or how many men we had with us. Then he went into a private conference with our commander.

"I don't know what they said, or what kind of deal they made, or even how Hastings could get away with that threat, since we didn't see any guns or any sign of an army. All I know is, one of our men was called into their conference room, and he never came back. Old Godfrey, he was the one that went. Some of the men thought it was because of his head, being so round and everything . . . round like a . . . well, a bowling ball.

"I think the old boy is a piece of athletic equipment now. Oh, well, nobody ever liked him, anyway. He smelled."

On the way to the boat, the soldier saw several people who had their left and right arms reversed. He said the people looked funny because "their arms reached around their backs instead of their fronts. We could never see what they were holding in their hands.

"I saw that dwarf with his head on backward again. I still see that guy in my dreams. It's real madness on that island.

"Our commander won't talk about it. The horrible thing about it is that they're all still out there on that island, performing God knows what kind of torture on people. And there's nothing we can do about it. Nothing at all."

BEAUTY MAKEOVER TURNS WOMAN INTO LIVING SKULL

12

It was a strange way to live.

It became a ritual. Get up. Make coffee. Sit down at keyboard in my underwear. Think of the worst possible thing I could think of.

It got so I had to play soothing music very loud and take long walks after writing the first drafts. As things got worse, I had to play Philip Glass music (which I like) extra loud as I wrote. *Einstein on the Beach,* which is fast and fairly insane, kept me from going over when I got close to the edge of the cliff. It took some part of me away from what I was

doing, or fed some better part of me that was being pushed down by the monster who was writing these things.

May I speak to Eve Black?

I couldn't figure out how this stuff was coming out of me. I knew I had a sense of humor. And I knew I liked "sick" humor when I was a kid. I even subscribed to the old *Mad* magazine knockoff *Sick.* But *Mad* magazine didn't go quite this far.

The Realist did, though. Maybe it had something to do with reading that magazine at a time when I was ingesting record amounts of LSD. Maybe all I was trying to do was to top Paul Krassner's piece in *The Realist* in which he describes Lyndon Johnson having sex with JFK's throat wound on the plane back from Dallas. Or was it the skull wound? It was written like a piece of investigative reporting, totally deadpan.

Do you think Krassner drove himself crazy writing that?

I remembered a particular feeling when I first read that at age nineteen. (Nineteen was younger then than it is now.) That feeling isn't so much different from how I felt writing these stories, or rewriting them now.

Of course, not all of my stories were horrifying. This one is.

BEAUTY MAKEOVER TURNS WOMAN INTO LIVING SKULL
by Judy Dunn

THERE IS a woman walking the streets of one of the world's great cities who will never let her face be seen by another human being again. That is because she has no face left to be seen — no face, and no hair. She is a virtual living skull as a result of a beauty makeover gone berserk.

She was an average, attractive woman, no beauty queen but pretty enough to have a couple of serious boyfriends. But that wasn't enough for her, and when she saw an ad for a $19.95 makeover, she called for an appointment.

She told us her story so that others like her would not be foolish enough to put themselves in her position. The victim, whom we'll call Suzie, should have known that the price for such an extensive service was too low, but earlier that day a young gorgeous secretary had started working in her office. The new girl was one of those tarts that boys like to hang around, a blonde with large breasts, a lot of makeup and a little swing to her hips.

Up until then, Suzie had been the favorite of the men in her office, so when the new girl started getting a lot of attention, Suzie decided to retaliate and take advantage of the outrageously underpriced makeover. It would be a decision she would regret for the rest of her life.

Suzie took half a day off to get the treatment, but she should have realized that something was wrong when she arrived. Workers were just installing the equipment. There were exposed electrical wires running all over the place, and there was an air of confusion. Suzie ignored these things because she was determined to recapture her status at the office.

After a half-hour wait, she was shown to a small room. A woman came in, smoothing her skirt and fixing her hair, acting as though she had just finished having sex, or at least making out. Suzie told her that she wanted to look sexier and that anything they could do to make her into a sexpot would be okay with her. The woman replied that she had come to the right place, and that if Suzie would just follow her into the salon the makeover could begin.

Inside the salon was a man in a lab coat soldering wires together. The woman introduced him as Jason and told Suzie that he would be giving her the makeover.

According to Suzie, Jason told her, "Looks to me as if you don't need too much work, but let's see what we can do." He looked her up and down and came within inches of her face, studying each feature and texture. He was handsome and Suzie was beginning to enjoy her visit.

"I think what we'll do first is give you our special Electro-Symbiotic facial and scalp treatment." She looked quizzically at him. "It's new, it's something I developed myself."

He brought out a large contraption that looked like a metal hood, almost like a diver's bell. He said, "Strange-looking, isn't it? But nothing to be afraid of. What we do is simply put some of this compound on your face and hair, and then you wear the bell over your head for a period of four minutes.

"You'll be able to feel some warmth while it's on. As you can see, it's got built-in stereo headphones and you'll be able to hear music during the treatment, okay?"

Hesitatingly, she agreed and he went about wiping the cream

onto her face, hair and neck. He put the bell over her head and fastened a tight collar around her neck. She asked if she could get out of this by herself if she wanted to.

He replied, "Not really. The bell weighs a lot and the collar has a lock on it for your protection, so that the treatment can be total. Well, here goes the music. Do you like that?" he asked. She shook her head yes as the sounds of repetitive New Age music filled the bell. "I'm going to go to the other room for a minute, but I'll be right back." He pushed a button and a motor began to turn.

"Don't go anywhere," he said, laughing. He hitched up his pants and said, "I've got a little unfinished business in the next room. Ha ha ha ha ha . . ."

Suzie could feel the warmth inside the bell. At first it felt good, but after a couple of minutes it began to get uncomfortable. Four minutes went by and Jason didn't return. Then five, then six minutes went by. The bell was getting very hot. The New Age music continued to play.

Ten minutes went by. Suzie wanted to take off the bell because it was so hot inside, but she figured Jason knew what he was doing. Five minutes later, she was screaming. She couldn't bear it, and Jason hadn't returned. Where was he? Did that remark he made when he was leaving the room mean he was going after the receptionist while Suzie cooked inside the bell?

By now she felt that if she had to spend any more time inside that hideous bell she would melt, she would cook, she would barbecue in there.

Suzie let out a long, bloodcurdling scream, the scream of a person being killed. It was so loud, Jason heard it all the way down the hall, where he was making furious love to the receptionist.

When Suzie woke up, she was in the hospital, unable to see because of the bandages over her eyes. When they took off the bandages two weeks later, she looked in the mirror and found she had no face and no hair; nothing was left of her head but the skull, teeth, tongue and eyes.

Suzie saw herself in the mirror only once. Once was enough. Now she walks around in a rubber Marilyn Monroe mask with a ski mask over it, so that it looks like there's a real face underneath.

She is on welfare because Jason and his lover disappeared that afternoon, after they discovered what had happened. Now Suzie is a penniless monster, unloved, unwanted, unseen, spending her days watching TV . . . all because she tried to be sexy and save a little money.

Doctors Transplant Nose from Her Face to Her Chest AND

BIGFOOT'S FOOT FOUND! GIANT SEVERED FOOT SMUGGLED OUT OF THE U.S.

13

What the hell was wrong with me? How could I write something like that? I was scaring myself. But then I would write a happier story like "Doctors Transplant Nose from Her Face to Her Chest" (it made it easier for her to breathe). And "Bigfoot's Foot Found!" (it was sold to the Prague Circus).

These were just silly. Cosmetic surgery meets an exaggeration of the medical advances in transplanting organs and such. It had to do with the image, the picture you got when you read the title. A nose on a chest. A lone, solitary Bigfoot foot. The word "foot" is funny. Noses are funny. Tings wit a "K" sound are funny. "Pickle" is funny. Oops, I was channeling the Sunshine Boys. Sorry.

I laughed when I wrote these. I laughed when they ran in the paper. I laughed when I wrote the headlines for the newspaper piece, and I laughed when I rewrote them for this book.

I am easily amused. If you've gotten this far, so are you.

DOCTORS TRANSPLANT NOSE FROM HER FACE TO HER CHEST
by Simon McAvand

IN A bold new move to cure asthma, emphysema, and other respiratory illnesses, a Bombay hospital has attempted to transplant a woman's nose from her face to her chest in order to help her breathe.

Dr. Rampal Thorepti, in a prepared statement, said, "We know this sounds off-the-wall, but so did the idea of heart transplants a hundred years ago."

At his news conference, he pointed to a drawing of a human figure and said, "We think that thousands of lives can be saved if the nose is relocated to the chest area. If the intake of oxygen occurs at the point of the lungs," he said, pointing to the middle of his chest, "there are a whole lot of things we can bypass.

"We can bypass the nasal passages. You know how stuffed up they can become. We can bypass the sinuses, the throat, the esophagus, too. This means that if food gets caught in there, people can't have their air cut off and suffocate.

"Yes, when the air goes directly from the new nose to the lungs, it is cleaner, and therefore more beneficial to the person breathing. If the air is cleaner, there is less in it to impair breathing, you know what I mean?"

Dr. Thorepti added that the woman, a secretary from the medical center, would have died from lack of breath if the nostriloplasty procedure, as he calls it, had not taken place.

"There is no doubt about it. It was a question of life or death. She was worried about moving her nose, of course, but cosmetic concerns just run a distant second to whether or not you're going to live. We assured her that in two to three months, we would be able to come up with an artificial nose to replace the one that is now in—or I should say on—her chest.

"What would you rather do? Walk around without a nose, or be dead?"

The doctor was asked if a simple hole in the chest would not have accomplished the same thing. He replied, "No, of course not. Anyone with a knowledge of physiology knows that the nose was invented for the intake of air. That's its only purpose.

"Why do you think humans have them? If noses were not necessary for the intake of air, evolution would have given us a big hole in the middle of our faces, instead. Sometimes these news conferences are a pain in the neck because of the ignorance of you so-called medical reporters."

He was asked how the nostriloplasty patient would be able to wear clothing. "Wouldn't a shirt or a sweater cover up the nose so that air couldn't get through?" asked a local reporter.

"That's a good question," he replied. "It is something we have tussled with. So far, we have developed clothing with a cut-out portion on the chest for the nose to come through. We feel that, as the operation becomes more popular, a whole style of wearing apparel will be developed utilizing the nose-in-the-chest design.

"I feel that seeing people walk down the street with noses peeking out of their clothes will not only be common, but will become accepted, and in time will become a fashion trend unto itself. After all, I think it's kind of cute. We all admire a cute nose, don't we? And to see it peeking out of a designer sweater is kind of sexy, don't you think?

"Now there's another question I want to get to because I know you will ask it. The question is, 'Where on the chest do we put the nose?' I know many women are modest about exposing any parts of their breasts. Well, they have nothing to worry about.

"The nose can be placed anywhere in a four-inch area. Higher up on the chest for large-breasted women. After all, we don't want the poor thing to smother, do we now? We put it lower on the chest for small-breasted women and women who are, you know, a little more daring.

"You see, medicine and fashion are very much interdependent

today. Although this woman is prepared to wait a few months until a substitute nose is found, we are prepared to go ahead with another operation in which we take the nose from a recently deceased person and put it where the original nose was, on her face.

"Why, you may ask, don't we just leave her original nose on her face, and transplant a different nose onto her chest? Very simple. Each person's nose is special. We are not using the new nose for intake of air; it is cosmetic only.

"In our early attempts at this procedure, we tried placing alternate noses directly onto the chest, and all of them were rejected. No, ladies and gentlemen, we have to use the nose of the person involved. It is the only way to get around these life-threatening respiratory diseases."

Dr. Thorepti's procedure has been pooh-poohed by several medical societies in his own country. It has been called dangerous, unnecessary and amateurish. One report called the procedure "sick."

"Dr. Thorepti has gone too far this time," it read. "We find this procedure to be outrageous and insane. We are going to sponsor legislation to outlaw such an operation."

In Bombay, the medical controversy rages, but Dr. Thorepti is standing by his theories. He has promised to introduce, in a few months, the woman who underwent the nostriloplasty so that the world can see that his operation is a success.

His critics say that even if the operation is a success, there is no reason to ever have it.

We will cover that news conference when it happens.

BIGFOOT'S FOOT FOUND! GIANT SEVERED FOOT SMUGGLED OUT OF THE U.S. by Steve Devlin

THE FROZEN severed foot of the legendary Bigfoot monster was discovered in the most remote area of eastern Oregon last week.

Reports from Marseilles, France, say that the foot is on board a container ship bound for that French port, and after that, is going to Yugoslavia where it will become part of the Prague Circus.

Inside information from entertainment sources indicates that the people who found the foot realized its entertainment value and offered it to museums and hospitals worldwide. The Prague Circus came up with the best offer.

The whole affair began when a pack of wilderness men were on a 200-mile hike through the vast Oregon forests. It was 19 below zero with a 50-mile-per-hour wind when the group walked into a clearing and saw what they thought was a tree trunk a quarter mile away.

As they got closer, they could see it was the size of an army tank. It was not a tree trunk, it was a huge, hairy severed foot with gigantic yellow curled toenails. It was frozen.

The men camped nearby that night, and talked about their find. One of them said to forget about it. Another suggested selling it for meat. Another wanted to build a theme park around it. But we have learned that Josh Marshall, a member of the group who found the foot, convinced the others to sell it as quickly as possible because nobody knew who owned the land it was on. He told them that somebody had to own it, and if they were smart they would steal the foot and sell it to the highest bidder.

While the arrival of the foot in Prague is eagerly awaited, anthropologists who have been studying Bigfoot for decades wailed in scientific indignation when they learned of the smuggling. Rodney Hillman of the Paris Institute for the Study of Bigfoot raged at the loss of the discovery.

"Imagine putting it in a circus! It is the one tangible piece of evidence we've ever had. All these years of sightings, pictures, movies . . . we've never had anything we could touch. Anything that would hold still long enough to have us examine it. What the hell does a circus want with it, anyway?"

Foot-smuggling mastermind Marshall is reportedly living it up in Rio along with his hiking buddies, living off the seven-figure deal they got, in cash, from the circus. His sister-in-law, Regine Marshall, who lives a few hundred miles from where the foot was found, told us that she had just returned from Rio three days earlier.

"Josh sent us plane tickets . . . me, his brother and the kids," she said. "We spent the weekend. As soon as Josh can get his businesses set up down there, we're going down there to live. Sure beats the hell out of 50 below where I am."

Bigfootomotrist Rodney Hillman complained, "Not only is this person living it up in Rio, but we can't even get up enough money to go to the area where the foot was found! Can you imagine? There he is, hopping around on one foot! Do you realize how easy it would be to capture him now? Suppose he's trapped? Suppose he's sitting somewhere up there and can't get around? What if he's starving to death at this very moment?

"Imagine what it must have taken to tear his foot off!!"

Indeed. The foot is so big it took a double flatbed truck to transport it to the ship that took it out of the country. Estimates are that it was as tall as a four-story building.

There are several theories as to how the foot got left there. One school of thought has it that since the U.S. government has been testing laser cannons in the Oregon wild, the foot might have been severed by a laser blast gone off course. Another group theorizes that it might have been a fight between two Bigfoots over a female Bigfoot. Josh Marshall's sister-in-law thinks it was dynamite.

"Yes, Josh told me it looked like it was blown off. Now, I know they were doing some blasting up there a couple of years ago when they were looking for coal, so who knows? Maybe he accidentally set off some leftover dynamite and blew his own foot off."

Officials of the Prague Circus would not comment upon their recent purchase. They wouldn't even go so far as to say they had ever even heard of the foot. But when we asked a number of circus people in Europe what they thought the Prague Circus was going to do with the foot, they speculated that it might just be put on display. Another said they might use it for people to picnic on in the summertime. A third thought they could make it into a vehicle for clowns to ride in.

"You know those little cars?" he said. "You know how they put a dozen clowns into one little car? Just think how many clowns they could put in that foot!"

Another suggestion was to hollow it out and make a swimming pool out of it, or fill it with water and freeze it so professional figure skaters could perform on top of it. Prague has been angling to host a Winter Olympics, and perhaps this could be a centerpiece.

But Bigfootomotrist Rodney Hillman thinks it's all a sacrilege. "It just drives me up the wall! To think of all that we might find out about the Bigfoot phenomenon! It makes me so mad!!

"At least we know where to look now. I hope we can begin our search in the next few weeks. Who knows? We might still find him alive!"

BAG LADY'S B.O. KILLS FIVE PEOPLE ON BUS

and

Woman Uses Taxis for Toilets:
One-Woman Wave of Defecation Terrorism

Even the stories that were borderline horrible but funny began to bother me, like "Bag Lady's B.O. Kills Five People on Bus" and "Woman Uses Taxis for Toilets."

I still couldn't understand how I could think of these things. Maybe I was possessed by Satan. It was better to contemplate that than admit I had the ability to think of this shit.

Any other reason was too scary. For instance, that I was mentally ill.

One component of the combination of delight and denial over this dubious success was my use of various pseudonyms. One for one type of story, one for another, some just at random, some combinations of names of friends of mine, some just out of thin air. Judy Dunn got most of the most horrific stories. Don't ask me why. I couldn't tell you.

BAG LADY'S B.O. KILLS FIVE PEOPLE ON BUS by Steve Devlin

A HOMELESS woman's body odor killed five people on a London double-decker bus last week. Police say the woman, identified only as Becky, slipped out the back door of the bus and escaped.

Autopsies of the victims revealed they had died of a rare disease found currently only in Ethiopian starvation camps. When a person hasn't eaten for a long period of time, the body begins to "eat itself." The waste by-products of this self-cannibalism are deadly to those who breathe them, but not to those producing the waste.

"It was Becky's flatulence," said the medical examiner. "You know, farts. That, and a combination of sweat and the fact that she hadn't had a bath for six months."

Becky had been a familiar figure around the downtown bus station. She had been a fashion designer, but after a long, difficult failed love affair, she had developed mental problems. For two years, people couldn't get her to stop talking.

"She just wouldn't shut up. She would talk for hours on end without stopping," said her psychiatric counselor. "She would just babble about anything that came into her mind. She lost her job, all her friends, everything. Nobody wanted to be around her."

After she lost her apartment and began living on the streets, Becky stopped talking altogether.

One of the conductors on the bus, Carl Weller, allowed her to ride for free from time to time. It was his bus she rode on the night of the deaths. Weller was one of her victims. At his funeral, Rob Dolley, a fellow conductor, described Weller as "a swell guy who would do anything for you."

He said that Weller had taken a liking to Becky, that he felt sorry for her. "He didn't mean nothing by it," said Dolley. "He liked all the bums and bag ladies. We warned him that one of them might stick a knife in his back sometime, but we never expected he'd end up getting killed by somebody's B.O.

"It's rough working on these buses, I'll tell you."

Police and health officials have been searching for Becky without success since the incident. They fear she will end up in a hobo camp and kill more people.

Reports of the incident say she boarded the bus and went to the top deck. It was there that the deaths occurred. Eyewitnesses say that Weller went up to check on Becky and was overcome by the toxic fumes.

When the bus pulled into its final destination, the driver expected Weller to meet him at the front of the bus. When he didn't show up, the driver searched the bus and found five bodies. "They looked horrible," he said. "They were all twisted up. They looked like they died in agony.

"Carl had a look of shock on his face. My guess is that he tried to ask Becky what the hell happened and he got too close to her."

Health officials are worrying that these incidents may become more frequent. In the United States, a panel of experts in the field of homelessness is meeting next week to discuss the problem. They feel that what happened in London could become an epidemic in America's large cities.

Liberals in the group feel that since funds have been cut off in the past few years, we may be in for many "Beckyesque" incidents in the near future.

"I'm afraid we may be seeing our streets littered with the bodies of people overcome by the body odor of the homeless and helpless," said one spokesperson.

Conservatives on the panel say that it's just something that we should let happen.

"We don't have enough money to take care of them. What good are they, anyway? They're bums, you know. They serve no productive purpose in our society. It's just evolution. We ought to just let them die off," said the conservative spokesperson, angrily.

Meanwhile, London police have made sweeps of the homeless hangouts. Next week, they plan to bring fire engines to those areas and spray everyone with high-powered hoses, hoping this action will alleviate the problem.

"If we could just get these people a bite to eat and a bath," said Roberta Singleton, of the London Welfare Board, "we could solve the problem."

But Becky is still on the loose. There have been no further reports of deaths caused by her condition, though there have been reports of a drastic decline in ridership on that bus line. Relatives of the victims of the tragedy are calling for tighter restrictions on bus riders. The father of one victim was quoted as saying, "I think we should treat these bums and bag ladies the same way we treat other forms of pollution.

"They should be outlawed!"

WOMAN USES TAXIS FOR TOILETS: ONE-WOMAN WAVE OF DEFECATION TERRORISM by Judy Dunn

"IT WAS a hell of a tip, brother!" That is the way a London cabdriver put it after he was the victim of the latest in a yearlong series of incidents in which a shapely American woman flags down a cab, takes a ten-minute ride and then jumps out without paying.

Losing fares is not an unusual problem, it's what she leaves behind in the backseat that has cabbies and police baffled.

"It's a pile of . . . well, I don't quite know how to put this for a family newspaper, but she leaves behind a pile of human excrement. Her own, we gather," said a police spokesperson. "She's done this thirteen times so far, once a month for the past year. She always picks different cab companies, different sections of London, different times of the month, different days . . . We think it's quite calculated. I think it's quite sick, if you ask me."

The cabbies concur. Lester Moran, a London cabbie for 20 years, told us, "I've never seen anything like it, and baby, I've seen everything. I've had fares have sex in the backseat. I've seen them change clothes, wash their hair. I've had them prepare whole meals back there. I've had fistfights, you name it. But this is the capper. This is about as sick as it gets.

"I picked up this girl near the train station. Nice-looking girl she was, too. Expensive dress and jewelry. I figured I got myself a nice fare and a tip to match. She tells me to take her to Savile Row so she can meet her husband.

"Better yet, I think. But when we got there she just laughed and jumped out of the cab and ran down the street into an alley. Well, I'm fifty-five years old and she was about twenty-five, so she just got away.

"So I'm sitting there cussing her out, and another woman opens the door to get in. But she only gets one leg in the door when she lets out this loud scream and says, 'Oh my God!! There's . . . there's . . . there's doo-doo on the backseat of your cab!!'

"I turn around and say, 'What the hell are you talking about?'

"She says, 'Look! There's . . . you know . . . doo-doo. A whole pile of it!'

"So she runs down the street and gets the police. I jump right out of the cab and open the back door and there it is, right in the middle of the backseat, a whole pile of it. The police came over and he looks in the back and sees it and says, 'How the hell did this get here?'

"I tell him about the bird who ran out on her fare. He says, 'Did she have a dog with her?'

"I say no, it must have been her.

"He says, 'Are you serious?'

"I say there ain't no other explanation, sir. I saw her moving around a lot and fixing her clothes, but when you've been a cabbie as long as I've been, unless they're trying to rob you, I don't pay that much attention to what goes on back there. I just try to give them a good ride and collect my money. Anyways, you don't figure somebody's gonna take a . . . well, do what she did in the backseat of your cab."

When the policeman filed his report, his sergeant called him in and said, "I just talked to the Chief Inspector about this and he told me there's no law against what happened in the cab. I said, 'No law?' He said yeah, but they're going to try to get one passed. Till then, if it happens again, you've got to tell the cabbies there's nothing you can do about it."

The law was passed three months later, but by then the woman had struck two more times. "We can't get a good description of her because she keeps changing her appearance," said a police inspector. "One time she's dressed like a punk, then like a royalty, then like a hippie. One thing's for sure, we know it's the same woman because we had her . . . uh . . . the . . . uh . . . what she left we had tested and it's from the same person.

"We don't know if she's doing it for fun or if she's got some grudge against taxicab companies, or what. And you know what else? We don't know if it's really a woman or not. London is full of female impersonators. Listen, if she'll go as far as to . . . uh . . . defecate on the backseats of taxicabs, what else could be going on in her mind?"

The cabdrivers' union has filed a protest with the Prime Minister because the police have been unable to crack the case. Arthur Firthington, speaking for the union, told us, "People pause before they get into cabs now. Since all this stuff began, we've had a drop in our ridership.

"Who wants to get into a cab full of xxxx? I sure as hell don't. People are starting to pass up taking the taxi, they're taking the train, they're walking, they're taking the bus. We've got to put a stop to this!"

Cabbies have begun taking precautions. Some won't pick up women fitting the descriptions of the woman in question. "Even with all the precautions, she gets away with it," said Firthington.

"We had one guy put an extra-wide rearview mirror on his cab, and she still got away with it. After all, you can't be looking in the mirror the whole time. Some of our passengers are ticked off about it. We've had women ask the driver to stop staring at them in the mirror.

"Now how are you going to tell the difference between someone who's offended by staring, and someone who wants to throw you off so they can leave a pile on your nice clean leather upholstery?

"I don't mean to make a joke, but this stinks. It really stinks!"

WOMAN GETS PREGNANT, HAS BABY SAME DAY

15

Conversations with Vader were interesting. I held him in some perverse awe. He was one of the kings of bad taste, and thus a kind-of hero to me. I always felt like my conversations with him must have been like those of two reformed alcoholics who had started drinking again. There were things you just didn't have to say. He knew that I knew how sick you have to be to make these things up. I knew that he knew that I knew.

He wasn't kind. He behaved like those people who know more than they want to know about the world and themselves. He was careful not to say too much. He never used the words "made up," or "lies," or "fake." Maybe he thought somebody was recording his telephone conversations. I sure wish I had.

He never put anything in writing, other than which stories he was buying and which he wasn't. Most of our correspondence was about money, pitiful though the money was. But he liked my stories enough to tell me that I was the only free-lancer who got paid on acceptance, and not upon publication. I took pride in that—it meant that my trash was worth something. What was I, nuts?

But our telephone talks always pointed me in the right direction. For instance he always wanted good birth stories, hence this charming item.

WOMAN GETS PREGNANT, HAS BABY SAME DAY
by Steve Devlin

A WOMAN made medical history last week, when she became pregnant and had the baby all in one day. Doctors say it was bootleg fertility drugs that caused the shortest pregnancy on record.

When Les Lauderdale came home from work, he found his wife being loaded into an ambulance. The attendant told him she was only minutes away from having a baby.

"But my wife's not pregnant!" he said, his eyes as big as saucers.

The attendant answered, "Oh, yeah? What do you think *that* is?" pointing to her distended stomach. "If you want to go, you better get in right now, because we don't know if she'll make it to the hospital before the baby is born," the attendant added.

When Les got in the back of the ambulance, he pleaded for an explanation from his wife, Jody. All she could say before the anesthetic took effect was "I don't know, honey. It all happened so fast."

The couple awakened that morning childless, doctors having told them they had no hope of ever having children. But at 7 P.M. the same evening, little Caprice Marie was born in what doctors describe as "a perfectly normal birth, very routine delivery."

The doctors didn't believe the couple when Jody revealed that the entire pregnancy had developed over the course of an afternoon.

"But it's true! It's true!" she told them. "We woke up at 6:30 in the morning and made love like we usually do. It's our favorite time of day.

"We stopped using birth control over two years ago, when the doctor told me I could never have children. After Les went to work, I went back to bed and had the strangest dream. In it I was pregnant. When I woke up around lunchtime, I had a big belly. I thought I was still dreaming, so I went back to sleep.

"I didn't wake up until five in the afternoon. I never sleep all day, ever, but when I woke up, I looked down and saw I was ready to have a baby!!"

Jody called an ambulance and then passed out. She was unconscious when Les came home and saw her being loaded into an emergency vehicle.

After an investigation, we have learned that Jody Lauderdale may have been taking powerful fertility pills purchased via the Internet. Independent medical experts believe she may have overdosed on these drugs in an attempt to conceive.

Dr. Nathan Holcome, of the prestigious Edinburgh Fertility Center, told us that if fertility drugs are taken in large quantities, a number of bizarre side effects are possible.

"It's quite unfortunate. In a related case, we found another woman who had been taking large doses of these drugs. She bore a baby with six arms and no legs. Birth abnormalities are common under these conditions."

Dr. Holcome went on to say that although he had never heard of a 13-hour full-term pregnancy before, nothing is out of the question.

When confronted with this evidence, Jody broke down and confessed that she had, indeed, been taking huge quantities of fertility drugs without her husband's knowledge. "Yes, I kinda figured they had something to do with it," she said.

But, she added, she couldn't be happier with the results. She has had no other side effects, and the baby is doing fine. But Dr. Holcome warns that taking fertility drugs without the aid of a physician is very dangerous and may lead to death and deformity. "Jody Lauderdale, by all rights, should be dead and buried by now," he added.

The new parents are thrilled to have their baby, but they say they don't recommend that anybody else do what they did. Jody says the horror of her one-day pregnancy will stay with her forever.

"Little Caprice Marie will help make it easier for me, but every time I look at her, I remember that trip to the hospital . . . not knowing what was happening to me, but feeling another life inside my body."

Les, the father, says he's a little disappointed that he didn't get to participate in his wife's pregnancy like a normal husband and father.

"I always wanted to take those birth classes and do all the little things for Jody that husbands are supposed to do," he said. "I've had to learn everything at once."

The Lauderdales have become celebrities. When word got out about her one-day baby, diaper services and babysitters came forward, offering their services for free.

There is talk of a movie, and maybe even a reality show where other wives take similar quantities of the drugs and are on camera for the next 24 hours, live.

"It's really too good to be true," said Jody. "But I think next time I'd like to wait the whole nine months."

WOMAN'S HEAD FALLS OFF AS SHE SLEEPS

16

Vader told me to locate my stories outside of the United States. This is why "Woman's Head Falls Off as She Sleeps" takes place in Italy. I never knew why he wanted that. I could never figure out why anyone would doubt that these stories were fiction. Who would first go check the location to see if it was true that aliens were keeping a bunch of kids in perpetual Christmas on a space station above earth?

I also enjoyed playing on the superstitions of the gullible idiots who thought this stuff was true. Like in the next story, where past-life dreaming, a popular delusion among my audience, was something meaningful.

WOMAN'S HEAD FALLS OFF AS SHE SLEEPS by Frank Burke

WHILE THEY were asleep, Carlo Tivoli reached over to his wife and cradled her head to his chest, just the way he always did. When he woke up, he found his wife's head still on his chest, but her body was on the other side of their king-sized bed. Her head had actually separated from her body during the night.

That was the story from mental health officials in Milan, Italy. Said Francesco Biagini, "We found it almost impossible to get her head away from him. He just wouldn't let go. He was holding it to his chest and crying, screaming her name over and over, 'Maria, Maria, Maria, Maria!!' You know, like that."

It took twelve men to separate Maria's head from Carlo's grasp. And when they finally wrestled it away from him, it fell to the ground and rolled into the gutter before anyone could pick it up.

The official said, "It was too bad. He was a raving lunatic already by then, but when he saw the head of his wife roll into the gutter . . . well, it will be many years before he will be able to be released."

The story has been pieced together from the accounts of friends and neighbors, and from Carlo's own wild ravings in the psycho ward. A police official told us, "We don't know how much of what Carlo says to believe, but a lot of what he told us checks out with the family and the neighbors.

"Maria had been having these dreams. Some people think she was reliving past lives in her dreams, but I don't know about stuff like that. So she had been having different dreams. One night she was Joan of Arc, next night she was Mary, Queen of Scots, then Marie Antoinette.

"For the three nights leading up to her death, she had been having a dream that she was an Italian noblewoman in the 1700s. I really can't recall her name, but people tell me it's popular. I'm too busy chasing crooks for nonsense like that.

"This noblewoman was unfaithful to her husband, so he cut her head off while she was in bed with her lover . . . in . . . uh . . . in the process, if you know what I mean. This is the woman Maria saw herself as, in her dreams. We can find nothing in her behavior to make us believe she was unfaithful to Carlo. To the contrary, she was totally devoted to him. My God, to her, every day was like a honeymoon. That's what makes this case so sad."

There is no scientific basis for the claims about what happened to Maria—people's heads just don't fall off their bodies while they sleep—but the police official, who is not a scientist, believes that it was the dream that caused her death.

"Look, the dream went like this. Maria, in her dream, has just met her lover in his bedroom. It is a very passionate scene."

We stopped him at this point, and asked how he knew the content of the dream. "Oh, she told it to her sister, to her upstairs neighbors, and to Carlo. When he puts enough words together to be understood, he spits out some nasty sex parts of the dream, especially when she gets the ax.

"See, the husband of the noblewoman knew she was going to meet her lover, and he followed her there. Oh, yes, my friend. The legend tells it that he placed a pig's head on their dinner table earlier that night. He kept looking from the pig's head to his wife's eyes and back again. Back and forth, back and forth, you know? We Italians can dream up some terrific tales, eh?"

The official told us that, earlier in the week, Maria had awakened just prior to the dream beheading in a state of total chaos. One second she is enjoying making love to her boyfriend in the dream and the next she looks up and her husband is swinging a silver ax at her neck.

"A very confusing situation, my friend," said the police official.

Carlo, her real-life husband, can't relate with anyone on a conversational level, but in his ravings, he sometimes tells the story of the dream and gives the doctors bits and pieces of what he found when he woke up that awful morning.

One of the doctors, who wishes to remain anonymous, told us, "We haven't been able to find out much. What we have learned is that the two, Carlo and Maria, had a little unspoken ritual in their sleeping habits. An hour or two before dawn, Maria would always wake up, turn over and put her head on Carlo's chest. They were a very close couple."

Maria's mother, Anna-Teresa Boldini, confirmed that. She said, "Oh, my God in heaven, she used to tell me how much she loved that man. You know how it is when a mother and daughter talk . . ." Boldini broke down in tears at this point and was unable to finish the interview.

The doctor told us, "The shock to the nervous system of finding the severed head of your wife on your chest upon awakening was so severe, this man may never recover. It's been two years and he still sees blood all over his hands and chest."

The police official agreed. "It was an awful sight. I hope I never see anything like it again. Her body was all the way over on the other side of the bed, just like she was sleeping. But her head was in his arms. They both slept nude, you know. Blood was all over the front of him. The doctors tell you he still sees it, eh? Well, I guess he does, I guess he does."

Police closed the case two weeks into the investigation. Maria's remains were buried in a Catholic ceremony, and her family wishes for her happiness in heaven. Carlo remains in the nuthouse.

Said the doctor, "To tell you the truth, he's driving us crazy. He keeps asking to be hanged by the neck so he can join Maria in heaven. That's what they did to the nobleman who beheaded his wife, you know, hung him."

ALIENS FORCE KIDS TO SPEND PERPETUAL CHRISTMAS ON SPACE STATION

17

As I rewrite these pieces, I notice things. For instance, I think the next story comes from someplace in my subconscious that was still dealing with a (real) TV story I did on conscious sedation. You know, where they give you drugs that make you instantly forget the medical procedure you're going through.

I remember visiting the office of the anesthesiologist whom I was profiling. He was also a dentist, and he also used conscious sedation on his dental patients. What I remember most was the screaming that came from the room in which he was working. It was the patients who were in pain. Pain that they would have no memory of enduring.

Why not make it happy for a change? In an icky way, of course.

ALIENS FORCE KIDS TO SPEND PERPETUAL CHRISTMAS ON SPACE STATION by Arthur Huxtabel

THERE IS evidence that aliens are keeping an entire city of Earth children prisoner on a space station millions of miles from home. A private concern that sends its own satellites into space has discovered this prison, which, sources say, is maintained so that the children think it is always Christmas.

This is done, according to Roger Walters, of Sussex, England, media spokesperson for the Underground Space Research and Development Consortium, by the use of an artificial gas. It works on a seven-day cycle on those poor kidnapped children.

"It's almost like 'Peter Pan,' in a way," said Walters, in an exclusive interview. "Every seven days they celebrate Christmas. Then while they are asleep on Christmas night, they are gassed again. This wipes out their memories, and they wake up the next day thinking it's a week before Christmas once again."

The clandestine organization stumbled across this lost village of Earth children during its own research. One of the Consortium's astronauts picked up something strange on his radio. It sounded like a group of children singing "Silent Night." The astronaut couldn't understand why he would be picking up such a signal, since he was far from Earth and his radio was pointed in the opposite direction.

Said Walters, "He maneuvered his spacecraft in the direction of the signal and found a space station. But as he got closer, he was attacked by lasers and driven away. Before he was attacked, he managed to receive video and audio signals from the space station.

"When he escaped the laser attack and was able to play back the tape, he was astonished to find it contained pictures of 25 Earth children, ages 6 to 10, real human children! They were sitting around a Christmas tree, opening gifts and having a wonderful time."

The tape was analyzed at the Consortium's headquarters and upon close examination, researchers discovered that the children were indeed human, but that the force controlling the space station was of an alien nature. "We concluded that these poor little kids were being held prisoner for some kind of fiendish experiment," said Walters.

The organization decided to direct a great deal of its energy to finding out what this was all about, but the next time they sent a spacecraft to look for it, the space station had disappeared. "We went back to where we had found it before," Walters explained. "We were armed this time—we had our own lasers and laser shields. Unfortunately, the Christmas prison had vanished."

Two years later, during a mission beyond the deepest point in space yet visited by man, the Consortium's spacecraft encountered the same signals, again little children singing "Silent Night."

"This time we were ready for it," Walters went on. "What we weren't ready for was what appeared on our TV screen at mission control. What we found was that it was the same children, at the same age. Remember, this was two years later, but the children had not aged at all. They were still the same, everything was the same.

"All of our scientists just sat and watched the scene unfold on our monitors. Many of them sat there and cried. Brilliant, hardened scientists cried at the sight of these poor children, caught in time, celebrating Christmas."

After the scientists regained their composure, they ordered the astronauts to maneuver closer to the space station. "We knew by then that the station was being run by remote control, because our sensors told us that the children were the only life forms aboard it.

"Our captain noticed a gas being released from the far side of the station, so he captured some of it, all the time fighting off a laser attack, which must have been triggered automatically. Believe me, it was quite painful to have to sit there and do all this while watching a room full of children sitting around a Christmas tree, singing 'Here Comes Santa Claus,' eating candy canes and laughing. All the while we knew that it was a cruel hoax, knowing it wasn't really Christmas, that it was really the middle of July!"

When the Consortium's spacecraft came home and the gas was analyzed, the scientists found a strange thing. "We put five people in a room on Christmas Day, and exposed them to the gas," said Walters. "Everything went along just fine. They opened their presents, had their Christmas dinner and then went to bed.

"But when they woke up the next day, they all thought it was the week before Christmas. They all wanted to do the things people do to get ready for Christmas all over again. We allowed them to do this in our labs, and one week later, they all celebrated Christmas again. This time they went to sleep without the gas and they woke up normally. They thought it was the day after Christmas.

"Our head scientist theorizes that aliens have been conducting an experiment on a group of our children. He says the aliens kidnapped them on Christmas Day and have kept them in perpetual anticipation and celebration of Christmas every seven days by using the gas on them. We think it's a way of testing humans so that they can be eventually made to work as slaves of these aliens.

"You know, if they give the gas to people every few days, they will perform the same tasks over and over and over with no questions asked. Meanwhile, we have plans to rescue these poor, innocent children, caught in time and unable to grow up. We're not sure how we're going to do it, because they keep changing the location of the space station prison. But we do know who these children are. We have contacted their parents, those poor people.

"They long to have their children returned, and we're doing everything we can to bring them back. The problem is, we're getting no help from the space superpowers. As a matter of fact, they are preventing the return of these precious kids.

"We're not going to give up. We've put aside all of our industrial experiments in space to try to bring home this perverse Christmas party. We think the future of all our kids, even of our planet itself, depends on it!"

IS DREADED BRAIN-EATERS DISEASE COMING TO THE U.S.?

18

The more of these I rewrite, the more I realize that one thing is becoming very clear. The methods I used to get to people are almost exactly like those used by Nazis, Commies, and many contemporary U.S. politicians and news networks. It's the big lie concept: the bigger the lie, the more they'll believe it.

The Rules:

First: Make something up. It doesn't matter how wacked-out it is, or how patently false to anyone with half a brain.

Second: Put it in a context that people are comfortable with. If it's for a newspaper, write it so that it really, really sounds like a newspaper story. One that's true. Same goes for TV. Best to have a distinguished-looking person read it, if it's on TV. He's not a journalist, but he plays one on TV. There I go, quoting Firesign Theatre again.

Third: Tell the story a lot. Play it over and over if it's for TV. The more you play it, the more people will believe it. The big lie, told often, becomes truth after a while.

Fourth: Pander to the worst in people. Work their fears, their ignorance, their perverse pleasures. A worst-case scenario always worked for me. Predicting a worst-case scenario has worked for politicians since antiquity.

Fifth: Quote somebody whom others don't know or will never check. Hardly anybody checks anything. It's better to jump on board the bus and run with an outrageous story. Some editors will just let things slide. Other editors or news directors have instructions from on high.

Sixth: Make them feel a very big emotion. Get their blood boiling. Make them cry. Gross them out. The ability to tell a story in a way that makes the audience react will keep you employed.

Seventh: Under no circumstances admit you were wrong or that you made it up. When someone comes at you with the real facts, call them names. Impugn their patriotism. Imply that they're mentally ill. Divert all attention from your story.

As H. L. Mencken (another malcontent from Baltimore) once said, "Nobody ever went broke underestimating the taste of the American public."

Let's get back to my appearance on *Oprah*. By now I was on a roll.

"Was there an ounce of truth?" Oprah asked.

"No," I said. "Well, once in a while. I did a story on kuru, a disease that only the cannibals of New Guinea get. And they get it from eating human brains."

There was a shot of a woman cringing.

"Now, that's a real disease. But I took it a step further and had the 'National Liberation Front of New Guinea' export it to New York City and infect homeless people as a terrorist act. You know, feed them . . ."

Murmurs.

"Unbelievable. Unbelievable," said Oprah.

Well, I would think so.

But it really did have some truth to it. I had just broken up with a nurse, who still liked me enough to let me in on a disease that actually exists, which she had read about in a medical book and couldn't wait to share with me.

IS DREADED BRAIN-EATERS DISEASE COMING TO THE U.S.?
by Judy Dunn

THEY CALL it "trembling with fear." Doctors call it kuru, the most dreaded disease in the world. It is always fatal. It is transmitted by eating human brains, and it may be coming to the United States.

Kuru began in the highlands of New Guinea, where it was the custom to cook and eat human beings. It is caused by a virus and takes one to three years to show up after a diseased brain is eaten.

The first sign of the disease is difficulty in walking. The difficulty is slight, at first; then you begin staggering like you are drunk or on drugs. Eventually walking becomes completely uncoordinated, and after a while the disease victim becomes unable to use her arms or legs.

We say "her" arms or legs because the disease occurs mainly in women. Women seem to enjoy eating human flesh and organs more than men do, in New Guinea. Also, men who practice cannibalism rarely eat the bodies of women.

For centuries, the practice of cooking and eating human flesh, viscera and brains has been the custom in New Guinea, and kuru has been a way of life there. The disease usually lasts up to two years before killing its victim in a horrible death. The victim becomes uncontrollably insane, but death results from ulcers or pneumonia.

In the past 20 years, the incidence of kuru has declined because the custom of cannibalism has declined in New Guinea. But Dutch physician Hans Blomqvist has sent out a warning that a cult of New Guinean terrorists has broken out of prison on the island and may be on the verge of launching a new round of the disease in the U.S.

Known as the National Liberation Front of New Guinea, they stand for a revival of the old customs of the island, including cannibalism, and the rejection of all Western thought and industry. The group is reported to number 17—12 women and 5 men.

The group is down in number from 20 because during their six-month stay in jail, they butchered and ate three members of their own organization.

Their leader is a woman named M'Taba Baranga, a charismatic lunatic whose favorite pastime is to cook up a human stew. She has been quoted as saying, "Why don't you Americans just leave us the

alone? We had a good thing going here. What's the difference? You eat cows. In India, they think cows are sacred. Koreans eat dogs. You think dogs are a part of your ###### family!

"We eat our neighbors. We like how they taste. You think that's insane. I think it's insane to eat a dirty, disgusting cow. Have you ever spent any time around cows? I'd rather eat a person, any day.

"Why don't you Americans leave us alone? We didn't ask you to invade our island. We want you out, and we'll do anything to get you out!!"

The group issued a communiqué after breaking out of the New Guinea jail. It read, "We, the National Liberation Front of New Guinea, declare war on the United States and Europe!! We will come to your countries. We will eat your citizens. We will force your citizens to feel what it's like to enjoy the native customs of our land. We will recruit a whole new generation of cannibals from your population!!! Long live our beloved country!!"

Dr. Blomqvist, who has spent nearly his entire adult life studying the native population on the island, says if the group is successful, it could lead to new outbreaks of kuru among the population of some of the inner cities of the U.S.

"You know," he says, "there are a lot of people who are starving in America—white, black, Hispanic, Native American. It doesn't matter. You never know what people will do. If it comes down to killing or being killed, as it does every day in some of your big cities, who is to say it won't come down to eat or be eaten?

"Then we are in real trouble when it comes to kuru. I've seen what it does to people. They act like they are drunk, but it's far worse than that.

"There have been studies done with monkeys, you know. Samples of kuru-infected brains were injected into the brains of monkeys, and yes, they got the disease, too. But the research hasn't proven anything. They still haven't isolated the virus.

"We thought we had the disease licked when we got most of the people of New Guinea to stop eating each other, but with this so-called liberation group springing up, well, anything could happen."

There is no evidence that the group has left New Guinea. They may have gone back up to the highlands; they may have fled to another island in the chain. Since the breakout, new funding has been found for kuru research. The latest try involves oral feeding of kuru-infected brain to monkeys, with little result.

Part of the problem is that it takes so long for the disease to develop. This group could go to any country and begin their terrible work, and the disease would not show up for two to three years.

"Yes, they could be at work, anywhere in the world, right this minute," said Dr. Blomqvist. "The results would not show up for years. A big problem is that this group refuses to believe their cannibalistic practices have anything to do with the disease. They think it's just a mental illness.

"Matter of fact, in the old days, many of those afflicted with the disease were treated with high respect. They seem to think there is some wisdom attached to the dementia that kuru produces.

"I wish we could get through to these revolutionaries. I'll tell you what I think they are. I think they already have it, kuru.

"I'm sure the government of New Guinea is doing everything it can to stop the spread of this group, the disease and the export of cannibalism to your neighborhood."

RABID NUN
INFECTS ENTIRE CONVENT

19

I visited Vader at the paper's headquarters in Florida. I thought I had been introduced to the guy Central Casting had sent over to portray him in a movie. Fifties, chunky, bad skin, greasy hair, a little too busy to visit, and an air of distance.

It was uncomfortable talking with someone whose mind was even more twisted than mine. I was glad he didn't want me to be his friend.

I wrote this stuff for six months. I never ran out of ideas. I ran out of the urge to wake up and think of really awful things. People have asked me, in interviews and at parties, what was the most outrageous story I ever wrote for *The Sun*. Usually I tell them it was the Rabid Nun story.

RABID NUN INFECTS ENTIRE CONVENT by Theon Schwartz

WHEN THEY finally cornered her, she was snarling, howling and on all fours in her nun's habit. They had to throw a net over her and shoot her with a powerful drug in order to stop the horror.

By that time, Sister Casey Bond had left a trail of violence and wiped out her convent with dreaded rabies. All the nuns there, and the support staff, and the priests were all victims of her disgusting infection.

Many of them lie in hospital beds, frothing at the mouth, or receiving painful treatments with long needles in their abdomens. Others lie in graves, victims of Sister Casey's venomous bites.

Sister Casey had been the most beloved of all the nuns in St. Dymphna's Convent in Cefalu, Italy. She was known as the quietest, most soft-spoken, even most poetic of the 150 nuns. When she walked through the town, children would come to her, laughing. Dogs would run up and lick her hands. Cats would see her and begin purring. Even the birds seemed to sing more sweetly when she was around.

Her garret in the top of the convent tower was a haven for all those seeking peace and solace. Birds would fly into her window and sit around the room, never fearing her. When another nun or priest had a problem, they would come to her room and seek her out. Sometimes she wouldn't even have to say anything to them. Just being near her would heal them.

It was this attraction to all living things that was Sister Casey's undoing. Since she befriended all living things, she also befriended the bats that flew around the garret. She even recognized them, giving one the name Jack.

From her hospital bed, Sister Karen talked with us on the phone about what happened. "Jack was her favorite bat. I know that some people think that bats are disgusting and ugly, but Sister Casey had such a wonderful, peaceful way about her that she could not bring herself to hate another living creature. It just wasn't in her.

"She fed Jack, talked to Jack, even let Jack sleep in the same bed with her. He even went under the covers when the sun came up. I could never do that. I love God and all his creatures, but a bat is a bat. I mean, you wouldn't expect a person, no matter how faithful, to befriend a man-eating shark, would you?

"I'm not sure what happened. I have heard that the bat got rabies from another bat away from the convent. But all I know is that one morning, Sister Casey came down to breakfast with a bite on her hand. She was very upset. She told me, 'Jack bit me. I don't understand it. We love each other. He just flew in the room this morning and bit me. I was wondering where he was last night. The birds had gone to sleep but Jack didn't show up for his dinner. Then he flew in the window just before dawn and woke me up. His teeth were in my palm. Then he flew away and I haven't seen him yet.' "

Police say that this was the fatal bite. There is evidence of rabid bat venom in the small wounds in Sister Casey's palm. They say the wounds went untreated for a week, and the awful infection spread throughout her body.

Sister Karen told us that three days after she complained about the bite, Sister Casey began acting strangely. "I've never seen symptoms from rabies, but she began walking around with a napkin in her hand, wiping her mouth repeatedly, like she had drool coming out. She said she hadn't seen Jack since the morning he bit her. She missed him. But when she said it that third day, she had a little snarl in her voice that I had never, ever, ever heard before.

"Two days later we went up to her room to check on her and saw that she was gone. What we found, though, I will never forget. The room was full of dead birds. Some were dead as though they had caught some kind of disease, but some had their heads bitten off. Sister Casey was nowhere to be found.

"Later that evening, when the nuns were assembled for dinner, Sister Casey burst into the room, frothing at the mouth, raving and screaming, with her habit in disarray. I couldn't understand what she was saying. It sounded like gibberish. Like 'rollama-mollamyaconnabasindica-connabasathaba-kahnga.' I don't know what it was, but it sounded like Satan's language.

"She jumped up on the long dinner table, stripped off her habit and began biting people. Nobody could stop her. It was as though she had gotten superhuman strength. When she had bitten everyone, she ran out of the door, laughing and screaming."

Shortly after that the nuns began coming down with rabies. The first ones did not receive treatment in time and, unfortunately, died an awful death. Others, like Sister Karen, may recover.

The police combed the forest nearby and finally captured Sister Casey, who by then was like a wild animal. For some reason, which is currently baffling doctors, she has not died of the rabies. She is being studied by researchers from all over the world, who have convened on the prison where she remains in restraints.

There are times when the mournful wail of "Jaaaaaaack!!!" can be heard throughout the prison compound. The guards just look at each other and shake their heads. It's just poor Sister Casey, the nun who loved creation, in her perpetual agony.

MOTHER BITES OFF OWN TONGUE TO FEED STARVING CHILD IN ETHIOPIAN CAMP

I lied when I told Oprah that the Rabid Nun story was my most outrageous. It's not even close. It's almost too embarrassing to admit. Okay. Okay. Here is the story that helped end my tabloid career, and will probably send me to hell.

MOTHER BITES OFF OWN TONGUE TO FEED STARVING CHILD IN ETHIOPIAN CAMP by Roberta Gardner

"THERE AREN'T any stars in a famine. If Michael Jackson was here, he would be starving like anybody else, and no singing or dancing could help him. The things I've seen here will stay with me for the rest of my life."

Those are the words of Linda, a volunteer in one of the Ethiopian famine camps. She requests that her last name be withheld, and we sympathize with that.

"I saw a mother bite off her own tongue and try to feed it to her starving daughter. I can hardly talk about it. I was about twenty yards away. I happened to look up just as she tried to bite her own tongue off.

"She couldn't do it all in one bite. It took her several bites before her tongue was severed. I didn't react at first, I couldn't make my mind believe what I was seeing.

"Then she tried to feed it to her daughter, but her daughter wouldn't take it. She was only six months old, but she wouldn't take it, even though she was starving. Blood was pouring out of the mother's mouth.

"When the baby wouldn't eat the tongue, the woman went berserk and began running away. She really couldn't scream, though, because she had no tongue left, and because of all the blood that was pouring out of her mouth and into her lungs.

"We're not sure if she bled to death, or choked on her own blood, but we know she died. It's a good thing the baby wouldn't take the tongue. If she had eaten it, there would have been an epidemic of mothers and fathers biting their tongues off. I'm sure of it.

"See, this kind of stuff happened all the time. I put in my three months there, as a volunteer. I tried to do what I could, and if any of your readers want to volunteer, I urge them to do so. If you can help these people, please do. I beg you!"

Linda had been in the worst of the Ethiopian famine camps, and then was transferred to the bush. Her superiors wanted her to help the people who were so bad off, they hadn't been able to make it to the dreaded camps.

"The thing that struck me, even more than the horror I saw, was the fact that I knew that if this kind of famine had occurred in the United States, the same thing could have happened. I mean, there had been a whole village of people, we were told, that had set up a system of scheduled cannibalization. They had a schedule of who was to be served dinner, and who was to be served *as* dinner.

"Now, that may sound funny to you, but it's not a joke, believe me. A neighboring village wiped them out when they found out what was going on. It was a real holy war. The neighboring village leaders thought it was totally unacceptable. They thought it was murder and carried out capital punishment on the members of the village who had butchered and eaten their family and friends.

"Oh yes, their families. In order to get in a food cooperative, and be able to draw fresh human meat whenever they wanted, they had to give up a member of their family to be slaughtered.

"Yes, it's insane, and they were insane, but they were also faced with certain death by starvation if they didn't do something. Remember, these are people who couldn't even get to the starvation camps, where it was so bad people bit off their own tongues. These people were worse off than that.

"How could they eat it? Don't ask me. I was told that everything went into a community store, like. You know. So when you sat down to dinner, I guess you didn't know who you were eating. I guess it kept them alive, but it really doesn't make up for the fact that you're eating another person.

"You should have seen them. You know how those starving people look, you've seen them on TV, right? Well, this village was all plump and healthy. No bloated bellies. But what they did to get that way, it's horrifying."

After two months, Linda was sent back to the camp, where some of the same things had been going on. Not widespread, but enough to set everyone there into a panic.

"A gang would run through the camp at night, you know, crouching down and going really fast. Those famine victims, they can't react very quick, so when one of these scavengers came up and snatched a baby away from its mother, she wouldn't have the strength to fight back.

"We found places where little parties had been held. We found remnants of a fire, and yes, my God, we found little bones, skulls. It was like, you know, when somebody's really hungry and they eat a piece of chicken? And they clean off the bones? That's how it was with those little babies.

"They told us it was monkeys, but monkeys don't live there. There was nothing we could do—we're not the police, you know.

"I don't know how much longer I can sit here and talk about this," she told us. "It makes me sick to think about it. Doesn't it make you sick?

"But like I told you, if this had happened anyplace in the United States, people would have acted the same. North, south, east or west, people will eat anything rather than starve. Some people will, anyway. I mean, put yourself in their place. What would you do if you were starving? If you were going to die tomorrow if you didn't get anything to eat? Or your children? I mean die, drop down dead, and you knew it?

"And suppose someone offered you a piece of meat, and you knew it was human. What would you do? I don't care if you're from New York, Baltimore, Portland or wherever. What would you do? Better still, what would your next-door neighbor do?

"I know it's out of the news now, but things haven't gotten all that much better. We did all we could. I just hope more Americans will volunteer to go over there and do their bit to help humanity out of this horrible situation. It is my fondest hope."

VILLAGERS AT SHRINE WORSHIP STATUE OF ELVIS

That did it. By now I was unable to work on this stuff for more than a couple of hours at a time. With loud music blaring, so as to dampen my own realization of what had come, was coming, and would continue to come out of me, I would write the first draft and then immediately run out the door and take a walk.

My own imagination had driven me nuts.

So much for self-discovery. Don't let those self-help gurus fool you: it *is* possible to know too much about what's in your own brain.

It had nothing to do with fooling people. It had to do with wanting never to become Marilyn Manson. I couldn't admit that in public though, and I kept my smartass attitude with Oprah till the end.

"So how do you feel about yourself when you write that stuff and know that people pick it up and read it?" asked Oprah.

"If somebody is gullible enough to believe that a bunch of South American Indians who had never seen the outside world were discovered dancing around a nude statue of Elvis and chanting something that sounded like 'Viva Las Vegas' . . . I have a used car for 'em. . . ."

Laughs and applause. My time was up. Not a bad day's work, even if I didn't get paid for it.

VILLAGERS AT SHRINE WORSHIP STATUE OF ELVIS
by Judy Dunn

EXPLORERS SEARCHING for oil in the remotest part of the Peruvian jungle stumbled upon a tribe of Indians worshipping a statue of Elvis Presley. The strange thing is that there is no way they could have ever known about Elvis, because meeting the explorers was their first contact with the outside world!

A team of engineers was making their way through an uncharted part of the jungle in central Peru when they came upon a village made up of about 20 huts and one larger structure. They found 65 Indians worshipping a statue of Elvis inside the larger building. According to Rex Vosa, one of the engineers, it was a once-in-a-lifetime experience.

"We were lucky we stumbled on that village when we did, because we found out later that after they worship the statue of Elvis, they take it into the jungle to a secret place and hide it until it's time to worship it again."

The villagers were gathered in a circle around the nude statue of Elvis. They were making signs with their hands and chanting something that eyewitnesses swore sounded like the chorus to the title tune from Elvis's movie "Viva Las Vegas."

"It was the damnedest thing!" said Vosa. "We were their first contact with the outside world and yet there was an eight-foot statue of Elvis Presley and then this chant. This is one for Margaret Mead, or the Psychic Friends Network," he said with a laugh.

Although there were no anthropologists on the expedition, several universities have applied for grants to study these villagers, based on the photos and sketches brought back from the scene.

In the meantime, to help unravel this mystery, we asked the

famed occultist Gay-Darlene Bidart to theorize about how this could have happened.

"I have two theories about that," she said from her luxurious apartment on the Upper East Side of Manhattan. "The first concerns the tremendous sexual energy that Elvis possessed. It could be that, unknown to us, he was able to project his sexual energy anyplace in the world and reproduce himself. Do you know what I mean?

"He could have had the ability to lie in bed and project a map of the world on the ceiling and just point to anyplace in the world and re-produce himself. Remember, it was his sexual nature, his sexy wiggles and the way he carried off that macho sensuality, that made him famous. It was a rare thing."

In addition, Bidart feels that Elvis may have been a reincarnation of a figure in the "creative unconscious" of humanity.

"Go visit the Toltec ruins in Mexico, then go visit the ruins in Egypt. The Toltec gods look like Elvis. Elvis has, indeed, been a part of many cultures, not just 20th-century American culture. If you look hard enough, you can find him as part of the Egyptian dynastic iconography.

"It's all very complicated, but if you dig a little and use your imagination, you can find Elvis in all the ancient cultures. So it's not surprising that he turned up in South America, and not so surprising that a statue is being worshipped in Peru, of all places."

The engineers were able to communicate to the natives through their guide. They told the oilmen that the name of the god they worship was Ngeva, and that he was the sun god. Ironically, the name of Elvis's first record label in the U.S. was Sun, based in his hometown of Memphis—Memphis, Egypt, also being the place where Ramses II was buried.

"We asked them where they had gotten the statue," said Rex Vosa, "and they told us their ancestors had made it. We asked them how long it had been in their village and they told us it had been there for centuries."

The statue was made out of a strain of Peruvian marble found in that region. It was meticulously carved and was light brown in color. Oddly, although the Indians of the village have the normal facial features of the tribes in that part of the world, the face of Elvis looked nothing like them. It looked like Elvis. It even had sideburns.

We asked the noted phoneticist Arthur Cole to explain the chanting of "Viva Las Vegas" by the villagers. He said he wasn't so sure that's what they were chanting.

"I know it sounds like 'Viva Las Vegas,' but I think what you are hearing are the sounds of 'Viva Las Vegas,' but in reality the words they are chanting mean something entirely different in their language.

" 'Viva Las Vegas,' in their native language, means 'Hail to the God of Sun and Rock.' I know it sounds like a strange coincidence, but it's too strange not to be true."

Engineer Rex Vosa told us that the villagers are a happy bunch. "Oh, hell, they have a wonderful time. I don't think they're missing a thing by not leaving the village. I know it may sound strange to you, but they are very satisfied dancing around a nude statue of Elvis Presley.

"I think he would have liked it. I don't care how it got there. I don't really think they need civilization that much. After all, in America, wasn't it civilization that killed Elvis?"

When the engineers return to the village to begin drilling for oil, the team is planning to carry Elvis merchandise along with them. They'll be bringing ceramic statues of Elvis, sofa-sized velvet paintings of The King, Elvis-shaped wine decanters, and some of his biggest records, including the soundtrack from "Viva Las Vegas."

It should be quite a shock!

I'M NOT SURE WHETHER OPRAH EVER REALLY REMEMBERED ME FROM THE STA-
tion in Baltimore where we had both worked. By the time I did her show, I
was working for an ad agency that produced screaming car commercials. I
was comfortable there. It was work quite like writing fraudulent stories in a
tabloid newspaper.

My freelance tenure ended when it was obvious I was losing my will to
conceive these things, and when they got tired of me griping about actually
wanting to get paid. Winter in Baltimore is not fun, especially when you run
down to an empty mailbox every day expecting money to be there. I know
that's the fate of freelance writers, but knowing that doesn't ease the pain.

Vader finally sent me this:

*The last straw came when you wrote us a letter screaming for
money for stories which arrived three days later. The other stories
were vouchered the week they were received and payment is being
processed and will arrive shortly.*

Happy New Year!

I love that. He fires me and wishes me a happy new year. Totally in the role.

I don't think he was telling the truth about the stories arriving after I screamed about getting paid for them. But who do you believe, me or him? At least I have a tape of *Oprah* to prove I was on it. Everything else is conjecture, isn't it?

Anyway, when the end came, I was relieved. Plus, I had gone back to my TV job, so I didn't have to rely on the darkest parts of my soul for the rent.

But ever since then, I have wooed women with these stories. Readers from all over America have fallen to their knees in laughter at these jokes.

Just like you did.

ABOUT THE AUTHOR

TOM D'ANTONI is a writer, TV producer/reporter, and radio talk-show host living in Portland, Oregon. He has written for many national publications and newspapers. The tabloid stories for *The Sun* were made up; all of his other journalism is true. Really.

ABOUT THE TYPE

This book was set in Times Roman, designed by Stanley Morrison specifically for *The Times* of London. The typeface was introduced in the newspaper in 1932. Times Roman had its greatest success in the United States as a book and commercial typeface, rather than one used in newspapers.